D1462374

Praise for
IT's About Patient Care

Long before the Affordable Care Act (ACT) catalyzed a digital revolution in healthcare, C. Martin Harris, MD, and his colleagues at Cleveland Clinic were leading the way in technology-enabled, integrated, patient-centric care designed to deliver optimal clinical outcomes. *IT's About Patient Care* leverages these experiences to provide a uniquely informed view of what's next in Healthcare IT.

—DANA MEAD, Strategic Advisor at
Kleiner Perkins Caufield & Byers

In *IT's About Patient Care*, C. Martin Harris, MD, one of the world's most respected hospital CIOs, offers deep insight into the power of IT to support patients and caregivers. Under his leadership, information technology at Cleveland Clinic accelerates the transformation to value-based healthcare. Dr. Harris's insights enable the use of technology to build trust and relationships rather than depersonalize services or frustrate physicians. The Internet of Healthcare is key to enabling local delivery of world-class care to patients throughout the nation and beyond.

—ELIZABETH TEISBERG, PhD, Professor of Community and
Family Medicine at the Geisel School of Medicine at Dartmouth,
Senior Institute Associate at the Institute for Strategy and
Competitiveness at Harvard Business School,
and coauthor of *Redefining Health Care*

As we progress steadily toward a world of data-driven methods for maintaining wellness and treating health issues, the work done at Cleveland Clinic builds a solid foundation supporting this critical transformation.

—CRAIG MUNDIE, President of Mundie & Associates and former
Chief Research and Strategy Officer of Microsoft Corporation

The electronic medical record has been one of the most polarizing technologies in medicine, alternatively characterized as "savior" and "destructor." In *IT's About Patient Care*, Dr. Harris captures more effectively and simply than any other the very essence of what the electronic medical record is about: people. Delivering critical messages in an accessible style suitable for the techie and the novice alike, this book is a must-read for every healthcare consumer, practitioner, leader, and policy maker.

—RONALD A. PAULUS, MD, President and CEO of Mission Health

IT's About Patient Care performs a Herculean feat by portraying the transformation of healthcare not only at a systems level but also at the level of the individual practitioner. The reader witnesses the changes in both Cleveland Clinic and in the lives of its individual physicians and patients due to the gradual but systemic rollout of information technology applications.

—LAWTON ROBERT BURNS, PhD, MBA, Professor of Management
and Chairperson of the Health Care Management Department
of the Wharton School at the University of Pennsylvania

Having worked with Dr. Martin Harris and the Cleveland Clinic for over a decade, I can attest to the fact that the concept of patient care buttressed by the incredible advances in technology are in perfect harmony in that world-class facility. Cleveland Clinic today is twenty-first-century patient care at its very best. Dr. Harris has captured the essentiality of both technology and patient care brilliantly.

—GENERAL JAMES L. JONES, Former National Security Advisor
to the President of the United States, former Supreme Allied
Commander Europe and Combatant Commander USEUCOM,
and 32nd Commandant of the Marine Corps

IT's About Patient Care

Transforming Healthcare Information Technology the Cleveland Clinic Way

C. MARTIN HARRIS, MD
AND GENE LAZUTA

Mc
Graw
Hill
Education

New York Chicago San Francisco Athens London Madrid
Mexico City Milan New Delhi Singapore Sydney Toronto

1 2 3 4 5 6 7 8 9   DOC   21 20 19 18 17 16

ISBN   978-1-259-64293-7
MHID   1-259-64293-3

e-ISBN   978-1-259-64294-4
e-MHID   1-259-64294-1

Library of Congress Cataloging-in-Publication Data

Names: Harris, C. Martin, author. | Lazuta, Gene author.
Title: It's about patient care : transforming healthcare information technology the Cleveland Clinic way / by C. Martin Harris and Gene Lazuta.
Other titles: It is about patient care
Description: New York : McGraw-Hill, [2017]
Identifiers: LCCN 2016024454 (print) | LCCN 2016033035 (ebook) | ISBN 9781259642937 (hardback) | ISBN 1259642933 (hardback) | ISBN 9781259642944 () | ISBN 1259642941 ()
Subjects: LCSH: Medical care--Technological innovations. | Telecommunication in medicine. | Medical technology. | BISAC: BUSINESS & ECONOMICS / Management.
Classification: LCC R855.3 .H37 2017 (print) | LCC R855.3 (ebook) | DDC 610.285—dc23
LC record available at https://na01.safelinks.protection.outlook.com/?url= https%3a%2f%2flccn.loc.gov%2f2016024454&data=01%7c01%7ckari.black% 40mheducation.com%7c3553ab2fa0c14723756808d3b16e7cc9%7cf919b1efc0 c347358fca0928ec39d8d5%7c0&sdata=4YaE0zA2%2bBTSg055kQTpKrTQ m4vLFAOqAUpMS9qQKJ0%3d

To Susan, Jordan, and Evan,
who make the journey truly special
—CMH

This book, like every book,
is for my wife, Sue
—GL

Technology is changing the way we live. It ought to be changing the way medicine operates. And it is, at Cleveland Clinic. I envision the day, one day, when all of us will have our own electronic medical record that will be safe, will be private, and that will make healthcare more efficient.

PRESIDENT GEORGE W. BUSH
JANUARY 27, 2005

Cleveland Clinic has one of the best health information technology systems in the country. And that means they can track patients and their progress. It means that they can see what treatments work and what treatments are unnecessary. It means they can provide better care for patients. They don't have to duplicate test after test because it's all online. They can help patients manage chronic diseases like diabetes and high blood pressure and asthma and emphysema by coordinating with doctors and nurses both in the hospital and in the community.

And here's the remarkable thing: they actually have some of the lowest costs for the best care.

PRESIDENT BARACK OBAMA
JULY 24, 2009

Contents

Foreword by David Brailer, MD, PhD — ix

Acknowledgments — xiii

Introduction — 1

Chapter 1   A Digital Handshake at the Virtual Front Door — 15

Chapter 2   Vertical Thinking in the Mouse Museum — 45

Chapter 3   High-Tech, High-Touch — 77

Chapter 4   Electronic Health Record: Functionality, Adoption, Future — 115

Chapter 5   The Internet of Healthcare — 165

Epilogue — 195

Notes — 203

Index — 216

Foreword

The U.S. healthcare system has entered the second decade of a sweeping revolution in how information is collected, stored, shared, reasoned with, and used to guide diagnosis and therapy. Digital medicine is now commonplace in hospitals, physicians' offices, and many other sites of care. It is unheard of to treat patients without using an electronic health record today.

Despite billions of dollars spent and rapid technology adoption, the digital transformation of healthcare has a long journey ahead to realize value for our nation. Foremost among the goals is to apply the vast amounts of electronic data that is now being collected in ways that demonstrably improve patient care. Too often, digital data is locked away, no more accessible or usable than the reams of paper it replaced. Growing volumes of data generated from or by patients isn't collected or monitored by clinicians in a predictable manner. In most settings, digital data doesn't follow the patient throughout care, isn't compiled and analyzed so key trends can be highlighted, and rarely is used in public health and scientific research. Communications among clinicians and between clinicians and patients have not leapt into the digital realm in most instances. In short, patient care is like it has been for decades—yes, electronic, but not transformed.

In some institutions, chief among them Cleveland Clinic, the power of digital medicine is being intensively pursued, and it is changing care delivery. I visited Cleveland Clinic with President George W. Bush at the outset of the nation's health information technology effort. What has happened since has been dramatic. Minute-by-minute care of inpatients with highly complex conditions is orchestrated by digital communications. Patients in outpatient settings across the world can access top specialists as if they were next door. Health status is monitored so caregivers often know about problems before patients do. Smartphones are harnessed as tools for making care more convenient and higher in quality. Institutions such as Cleveland Clinic are the beacons that demonstrate to the nation—and to the entire world—why the digital revolution is important and how it can bring about the goals we all have for healthcare: greater longevity, less discomfort, better value, and fewer hassles.

This book distills the lessons learned at Cleveland Clinic over the past 25 years into a single and useful reference. C. Martin Harris, MD, whom I met in residency and fellowship 30 years ago, was among the first physician information technology leaders. While I followed the entrepreneurial route, Dr. Harris joined Cleveland Clinic as its chief information officer and pioneered what has now become a required senior executive position in every healthcare system. In his role, Dr. Harris has been at the forefront of the major leaps in health information: quality measurement, teleradiology, consumer engagement, provider communications, workflow management, point-of-care electronic records, telemedicine, and many others. He has been a steadfast and relentless agent of change and has all but written the book—which now he has— on how information drives clinical, technical, and financial success. Martin Harris has few peers with his depth of experience, perseverance, respect, and results.

We are in the early days of digital medicine. As the current wave of electronic record adoption ebbs, the next frontiers of health information are coming into view. Large-scale data analysis, remote care delivery, real-time physiologic monitoring, personalized treatments, and robotics are some of the ways that the last decade of investment will have a meaningful and durable impact on human life. We should continue to watch and learn from Martin Harris and Cleveland Clinic as they lead the way to this promising future of healthcare.

—David Brailer, MD, PhD
CEO, Health Evolution Partners
National Health Information Technology Coordinator
U.S. Health and Human Services Department (2004–2007)

Acknowledgments

The work described in this book occurred over a period of more than 15 years and required the close collaboration of clinical, administrative, and information technology professionals representing the entire range of Cleveland Clinic's operating model and medical practice. Much of it was unique in our industry for its time. Consequently, it was often intensive, costly, and inherently stressful, particularly in the heat of the moment, usually following months or even years of effort, when a new system or physical infrastructure component was first switched on. Everything we did felt entirely new when we were doing it and affected everyone in our enterprise. Nothing occurred in isolation, so in a very real sense, we have every Cleveland Clinic caregiver to thank for being our partners, our advisors, our colleagues, and our friends. Nothing we accomplished could have happened without their support, counsel, patience, and good graces. To every Cleveland Clinic caregiver, past, present, and future, I would like to extend my most sincere appreciation and thanks—with particular gratitude to the members of our current Senior IT Leadership team: Lou Capponi, MD, Timothy Crone, MD, Christopher Donovan, Adam Fogelman, Mitchell Krieger, MD, Amy Merlino, MD, William Morris, MD, Mary Partin, PhD, Pam Piar, Maureen Sullivan, Joe Turk, and Robert White, MD. Thank you also to Nelita Iuppa, DNP; and to Heather Walker for everything she did to help make this book a reality.

Leading an organization as complex and demanding as Cleveland Clinic through a period of unprecedented challenge and change, while increasing both the quality and affordability of the care we deliver, is a monumental endeavor. Holding to a forward-thinking vision of a technology-enabled practice model and steering the efforts of thousands of caregivers toward that goal even as so many other priorities compete for attention and support is a testament to the commitment of our leader, Delos "Toby" Cosgrove, MD, and his unwavering dedication to placing our patients first in everything we do. His guidance and trust, from concept to completion, is the invaluable foundation that is helping make the future we imagine a reality for our clinical and administrative colleagues and our patients.

Finally, I extend my deepest regards to every Cleveland Clinic information technology professional. The demands of transforming a healthcare delivery system of Cleveland Clinic's character and standards are unrelenting and unending. Our transformation is an ongoing journey that will continue for years to come. The professionalism, vision, and devotion of the members of the Cleveland Clinic Information Technology Division—those who are present today, those who participated in the past, and those who will join us in this work in the future—represent the fire that fuels what I believe is the finest, most imaginative, and most dynamic group of health information technology professionals in the world. Just as you created the title of this book, it is your work that makes this book possible, and it will be your responsibility to write the future chapters that, together, we are only now beginning to imagine.

Introduction

❝ f you are ever in a situation where you cannot speak for yourself, your electronic medical record will speak for you." That's what I said on Thursday, January 27, 2005, from my place on a stage that had been so recently built that it still smelled of sawdust and glue. It was just one sentence in my 15-or-so minutes of prepared remarks; and while I couldn't possibly have known it at the time, I have since come to realize that it is probably the single most prescient sentence I have ever uttered; it is the one that has had the greatest impact on the integrated health information technology work we have done at Cleveland Clinic during the past 15 years; and it will, I am sure, continue to inform the work we will do for years to come.

Here's why . . .

Along with several others, I shared the stage with the president of the United States, George W. Bush, who was visiting Cleveland Clinic to promote a national initiative he had formally introduced during an address he delivered on April 26, 2004, when he announced that, "Within ten years, every American must have a personal electronic medical record."[1]

We were in the grand ballroom of the brand-new Intercontinental Hotel on Cleveland Clinic's main campus. Somewhere out in the darkness beyond the klieg lights was an overflow crowd of Cleveland Clinic employees, philanthropic supporters, political dignitaries, local residents, and, crucially since he would in short order become instrumental in the

1

next phase of the advanced technology work that thousands of Cleveland Clinic caregivers were doing, Delos "Toby" Cosgrove, MD, the world-renowned cardiothoracic surgeon who had assumed his duties as Cleveland Clinic's president and chief executive officer[2] in January of the previous year.[3]

The name of this particular town hall style event was "Improving Care and Saving Lives Through Health IT."[4] And according to the members of the White House advance team who had become my personal "handlers" since we were informed of the president's intention to visit our organization, the whole reason that I was on stage that day was to explain the benefits of electronic medical record (EMR) technology in a way that would be meaningful to the American public—which was an assignment that had been keeping me up at night for weeks.

This was 2005, and I was enough of an industry insider to know that public awareness about health information technology in general, and EMRs in particular, hovered at around zero. (Actually, according to a survey conducted the year before by an emeritus professor of public law and government at Columbia University, 29 percent of participants claimed to have "read something" about EMRs,[5] which, believe me, sure *felt* like zero.) Also, at the time, only about 20 to 25 percent of U.S. hospitals had adopted any portion of an EMR system, and for private physician practices it was an even lower 15 to 20 percent.[6]

Despite these sobering statistics, there were still plenty of credible sources maintaining that with, say, a 90 percent national adoption of integrated EMR technology, the American healthcare system could save an estimated $77 billion per year through increased efficiencies alone;[7] and that didn't include a whole range of other savings opportunities, like a potential $3.5 billion in avoided costs that would follow an EMR-supported two-thirds drop in the annual incidence of preventable adverse drug events.[8] There was chronic disease management in large patient populations; increased access to critical data for medical research; the potential reduction of disparities in care across widely varying geographic areas; and a lot of other really desirable—if speculative—stuff that significant portions of the healthcare industry, the federal government, and the health information technology (HIT) profession were beginning to believe could, as the town hall's title flatly stated, "improve care" and "save lives."

Admittedly, the numbers available at the time were based on a select group of early adopters and included some monetary estimates that required a certain degree of faith to digest. But overall, there was a burgeoning sense of optimism in the air that led some credible authorities to describe HIT as an emerging (if vaguely monolithic) entity that could potentially become the most significant transformational agent in the way medicine is practiced since French microbiologist Louis Pasteur, English surgeon Joseph Lister, and German physician Robert Koch postulated (and demonstrated the veracity of) the "germ" and "sterilization" theories in the mid-nineteenth century.[9]

But, predictably, there was another side to the HIT conversation in which the voices of some very experienced, very respected healthcare delivery system experts were making a cautionary argument around the projected disruptions a wholesale transition from a paper-based medical practice model to an EMR-enabled environment could potentially inflict on provider workflows,[10] resulting in a serious decrease in productivity that would (inevitably, it seemed) increase the cost of healthcare for both private and public payors.

So, while the public at large knew next to nothing about EMRs, good or bad, and the healthcare industry could not agree on what it knew about the same subject, I was being asked to briefly explain the whole evolving concept in clear, unambiguous language as my personal contribution to helping the president of the United States (who would be sitting right there, next to me on stage) advance the very healthcare policy priority his visit to Cleveland was meant to celebrate.

This was definitely *not* why I went to medical school.

During the three weeks leading up to the president's visit, our facilities engineering teams kept themselves busy by building not only the stage from which he would speak but, because he would not leave the building after it had been cleared by his personal security detail, a technology-connected, broadcast-ready demo operating room (OR)—complete with little hinged doors down near the baseboards for the bomb-sniffing dogs—right inside the hotel. While they were doing that, I was bouncing ideas off of a core group of cooperative colleagues, diligently writing and rewriting my remarks, sticking to the facts, staying focused on detail, saying nothing that didn't support my point . . . which is exactly where I kept falling down because it wasn't long before I realized that I didn't actually know what point I was trying to make.

Then I ran across, of all things, a story about one of Cleveland Clinic's founders, George W. Crile, MD, and my thoughts began taking shape. It was during a very late-night session in which our executive leadership team was reviewing, for about the ten thousandth time, all the information we were going to include in the press packets and other materials that would be made available to the media and other attendees of the presidential town hall event. Sitting at a huge oval table piled high with binders, papers, and test printings glued to stiff cardboard backing, I was languidly paging through yet another (seemingly unchanged) version of "A Brief History of Cleveland Clinic" when an unfamiliar section title caught my eye:

Dr. George Crile Stages Fully Mobile Surgical Hospital in Fairmont Park, Philadelphia, October, 1916.

Okay, I thought. This is new. So, I read:

At the request of the Surgeon General of the United States Army, George Crile, MD, a professor of surgery at Cleveland's Western Reserve Medical School, mobilized a full-scale, first-of-its-kind battlefield hospital, complete with horses, tents, surgeons, anesthetists and a support staff of internists, neurologists, dentists, nurses, and even stenographers, on Fairmont Park's manicured grounds.[11]

Dr. Crile, an internationally recognized authority in the treatment of shock, and the first clinician in the United States to successfully transfuse blood from one living human being to another, was determined to prove that his idea of bringing together medical experts from multiple specialties, supported by the latest medical technologies, in one efficient unit could significantly improve a soldier's chances of surviving the battlefield wounds inflicted during the world's first mechanized war as compared to the mostly improvised treatment that was, at the time, being delivered by well-meaning but under-trained and under-equipped medical personnel. His vision even went so far as to include an X-ray machine, and its accompanying mobile laboratory for developing film, right there in the field.

Dr. Crile's elaborate demonstration was so successful that U.S. Army, Navy and Red Cross officials spent days studying its design, which would eventually influence the organization and delivery of critical care all the way through to (as some informed people contend) the establishment of the now familiar Mobile Army Surgical Hospital, or M*A*S*H*.

In 1921, Dr. Crile, with three of his wartime physician colleagues, Frank Emory Bunts, MD, William Edgar

Lower, MD, and John Phillips, MD, established Cleveland Clinic on this same core set of multidisciplinary, technology-supported principles. Today, that tradition continues through the work of Cleveland Clinic innovators who are using integrated Information Technology systems to connect this enormously complex healthcare delivery organization into a single, efficient enterprise that is aligned around, and dedicated to, putting the individual needs of every single patient first in everything we do.

Maybe it was the lateness of the hour, or the unrelenting schedule of getting ready for a presidential visit while maintaining my duties as Cleveland Clinic's chief information officer; maybe it was something about the way the story was written. I am originally from Philadelphia, and I know Fairmont Park well. The image of tents, horses, wagons, and all the rest of what the audacious Dr. Crile had assembled there struck me. The effort it must have taken . . . the sheer amount of work . . . and that's when it hit me: the reason my previous attempts at describing an EMR to the general public had failed, and why the actual assignment was itself misdirected.

What George Crile—a man who, to this day, is remembered not only for his surgical skill but for a multitude of other accomplishments[12]—had done was nothing less than elegant in its simplicity: charge your best people, even those who may never have worked together before, with creating a truly multidisciplinary team capable of functioning at a really high level, give them the latest technology tools you have to offer, and put them where they need to be, when they need to be there, to do the most good for the people for whom you are providing care.

In other words, instead of transporting grievously wounded soldiers to where it was convenient to set up a hospital, put the hospital close to where the soldiers were actually being hurt.

To the classic organizational paradigm of people, process, and technology[13] Dr. Crile had added a fourth parameter that was screamingly obvious once you've seen it: *place*. By so doing, he created an operational philosophy that was so inherently practical that he had to physically make what he was proposing come to life in Fairmont Park so the army surgeon general (or anyone else, for that matter) would be able to visualize and understand it.

And now, reaching across almost a century, the good doctor had done the same for me.

An EMR was not about software, or hardware, or network systems, or baud rates; it was not about any of the technical particulars I had been trying so hard to describe. An EMR was about what it could do for patients . . . for people . . . for each of us as individuals and for each of the people we love. It was not about technology. It was about what you do with the technology and where you do it that must drive not only how you explain it but how you imagine, implement, and use it.

Is an electronic medical record important because it is contained in a computer instead of a paper chart filed away in a cabinet? No. It is important because it makes it possible for all your crucial information to follow you wherever you go so that any clinician who is called upon to render your care can access and use it to help guide and inform his or her decisions.

Following that same line of thought, for an EMR to deliver its greatest potential value, the information in it needs to flow, on demand, from location to location over a network capable of seamlessly connecting multiple systems. This allows caregivers representing a variety of critical specialties, using their own specialized equipment, to contribute their particular expertise to the group's coordinated work. And this same interoperable system—which is a system composed of devices that can exchange and interpret data[14]—by its very nature, could also be used for all sorts of other really important things, such as linking geographically distant medical science centers into virtual research consortiums capable of focusing the world's best investigators on overcoming miseries like Parkinson's disease and cancer that have dogged mankind for centuries.

So it was with a head full of warhorses, network schematics, wagon wheels, and Internet protocols that I drove out of our parking garage and headed for Hopkins International Airport. It was four o'clock in the morning, three days before the president's visit, and I hadn't slept all night. But I was scheduled to deliver a lunchtime talk to a physician conference in Chicago, and my flight left at six.

To get to the airport from Cleveland Clinic's main campus, I had to use the I-90 Innerbelt Bridge, a quarter-mile span that crosses over the "flats," a low-lying basin area near the mouth of the Cuyahoga River around which Cleveland's steel mills are clustered, their narrow black smokestacks jutting up into the predawn darkness. As I glided along, two exceptionally tall stacks exhaled a pair of blazing orange fireballs that flared up probably a hundred feet. They were so brilliantly bright that they briefly illuminated my car's windshield, revealing a sparkling mist of falling snow that had been invisible just an instant before.

I had a small, handheld microcassette recorder that I sometimes use to capture my thoughts when I am preparing for an important talk or meeting, and as the trembling flames were swallowed by the dark, I fished it out of the glove compartment, hit record, and set it in the cup holder.

"Imagine," I said, "that you are a 55-year-old man. You're in fairly good health, though, like many Americans, you do take medication for your high blood pressure, and a statin to control your cholesterol. But unlike most Americans, you are allergic to aspirin.

"Now imagine that you are on vacation in Florida. Leaving your wife on the beach, you decide to take a quick walk down to a local convenience store for some ice and a few cans of soda to refill your cooler. As you're crossing the store's parking lot, you experience a terrible blast of pain in your chest. You start sweating, the pain gets worse, and you wind up sitting on the sidewalk, leaning against the store's front door, gasping for breath. By the time an ambulance gets you to the local hospital emergency department, it's clear that you're having a heart attack, but by then, you're unconscious.

"Now, remember, you live in Cleveland, you're just vacationing in Florida. You're having a heart attack, and you're wearing swimming trunks, a *Bad Company* T-shirt, and flip-flops. All you have in your pocket is a wallet with about 30 dollars in cash, a couple of credit cards, and your Ohio driver's license. Your wife even has your hotel room key in her beach bag.

"So, what do the nurses and doctors who are going to take care of you actually know about you? Do they know that you have a history of high blood pressure and high cholesterol? No. More importantly, do they know that you're allergic to aspirin? No, they do not. And what's one of the first things they do when a patient arrives in an ED complaining of chest pain? They give you an aspirin—which in your case, with your medication allergy, would make your situation infinitely worse.

"And remember, your wife doesn't know where you are.

"But even if she were with you, what could she do? When the doctors asked her, 'Does your husband take any medication?' which they most certainly would, what could she say? Suddenly pressed into service as your walking medical record, she would probably reply with something like, 'Yes, one for his blood pressure and one for . . . oh, something with this diet. His sugar . . . or his cholesterol; I don't know. I'm upset. He takes a green pill, and he takes a capsule that's white and . . . red, I think; or orange. Is he going to be all right? Is my husband going to die?'

"And maybe she'd mention your aspirin allergy, and maybe she wouldn't, because, unless she knows that aspirin is a frontline medication in the treatment of heart attack, why would she even be thinking about it?

"As I hope you can see, this is not a unique scenario. Something like it happens all the time. As a matter of fact, something very much like it is probably happening right now. Right now, right this minute, I'm certain that, somewhere in this country, there are doctors basing important, time-dependent treatment decisions on information they would never trust under any other circumstance. And there are worried, fearful, and confused patients and their families who are doing their very best to remember the details of things that they just never paid that much attention to before.

"But now imagine that, as our patient, you have something else in your wallet. Imagine that you have a card that says that you have a Cleveland Clinic MyChart account, which means that, as a Cleveland Clinic patient, you have online access to portions of your own electronic medical record through our secure, Internet-based patient portal.

"Now, everything is different. Instead of making guesses around what they should do, your doctors can use the information on your wallet card to log in to your MyChart account and see everything about you. They can see your medications—doses, strengths, frequency, and prescribing rationale. They can see the conditions your physicians are treating; they can see your allergies; they can even see your wife's contact information so they can call her to tell her where you are.

"At Cleveland Clinic we have been working hard to build a technology infrastructure that connects the inpatient and outpatient sides of our practice in all of our practice locations. So today, at Cleveland Clinic, the story I just told you is actually true. It's a fact. If you were unconscious when you arrived in any hospital emergency department equipped with a computer, and you had your MyChart card in your wallet, your doctors would know you. You or a member of your family would not need to recite your medical history because your electronic medical record would speak for you.

"And that is really what we are talking about today. What the president is proposing is nothing less than a healthcare system in which no American will ever be a stranger to the people delivering their care. Because, with such a system in place, if you are ever in a situation where you cannot speak for yourself, your electronic medical record will speak for you."

There was more, but that is, word for word, what I transcribed and, more or less, what I said from the stage that day in 2005. Today, over a decade later, listening to that tape, I am struck by how much has changed since that dark January morning and, perhaps even more, by how much has not. I was able to listen to that brittle old tape one last time before it stretched and snarled, so my words from the past are gone for good. But their spirit still resonates in the amazing work thousands of Cleveland Clinic caregivers have done in the intervening years to make the vision I so optimistically described come true.

Other things have happened as well. In some ways, where we are as a nation in terms of reimagining our healthcare system in a new, technology-enabled way is great. President George W. Bush's electronic medical record challenge led to the creation of a new federal administrative position, the national coordinator for health information technology, first held by David Brailer, MD, PhD, a friend and colleague who kindly provided the Foreword to this book.[15] Then came the Health Information Technology for Economic and Clinical

Health (HITECH) Act signed by President Barack Obama in February 2009, which was designed to "promote the adoption and meaningful use of health information technology."[16] That led to a set of standards around what constitutes a "meaningful use" compliant EMR, which helped catalyze the subsequent increase in the number of physician practices and hospitals across the country that have begun implementing and using these systems.

But with progress came controversy and, often, discord. A transition of this magnitude is not easy. Longstanding, long-taught ways of working and thinking have been and are being revisited and reexamined. What today's new medical school graduates know about using connectivity tools to collaborate with their colleagues and to facilitate the functions and processes they require each day is very different from what their older, more experienced colleagues know and were taught. And the experience and, significantly, the *expectations* of the students who are only now embarking on their medical education will be so different in their turn that just trying to imagine them is intimidating—which is, coincidently, the whetstone that sharpens an exciting idea's cutting edge.

This book is composed of a series of stories about some of the most important successes and failures we have experienced during our journey to Cleveland Clinic's present state of technology enablement, tied together by a handful of critical concepts that are listed in Chapter 1, and to which we will return at opportune points over the course of this discussion. I hope that our experience at Cleveland Clinic will help our colleagues in the healthcare industry and those who use and pay for the services we provide better understand where we, as practitioners, payors, and patients, have been and where we aspire to go. Each of the following chapters concentrates on an aspect of our practice that has been significantly changed or, in some cases, entirely enabled by IT and other technologies.

We will hear from the caregivers who conceived and created the systems we describe. More important, we will meet a number of patients whose lives have been directly affected by the services that resulted from this work.

While this book may ostensibly be about technology, what it's really about is the transformation of the contemporary healthcare model that is happening all around us, right now. Nowhere will I argue that health information technology is *causing* this transformation because the true drivers of change are real-world financial concerns, an increasing demand by payors and patients to understand exactly what they are getting in exchange for the healthcare dollars they spend, and a growing focus on measuring and quantifying the quality of the care patients actually receive. But even if technology is not the reason *why* our care model is transforming, it is, I believe, the reason our care model *can* transform. Without the real-time data access and analytic capabilities HIT systems deliver to the clinicians and administrative professionals who design and operate our healthcare organizations, we would not have the increasingly detailed perspective on the work we do and how we utilize and distribute our resources that we need to make the kind of foundational changes that will lead to real progress. Without the connectivity capabilities today's HIT systems deliver, we could not even imagine some of the innovative solutions that are, regardless of physical location, quickly connecting the right patient and the right specialist, whether it is through online second medical opinions, or face-to-face video visits supported by integrated medical devices and secure, high-speed Internet connections. And without the creative palate that today's HIT systems represent, many of the most promising ideas generated by some of our most imaginative innovators would never be realized.

With a rational understanding of what HIT can realistically do today and a shared vision of the healthcare system we would all like to build for tomorrow, I believe that we can use the power of this technology to make our work more efficient, reduce unnecessary expenses that contribute to the cost of care, and speed up the process of bringing the right patients and the right clinicians together so the healing that starts with human contact can begin.

A Digital Handshake at the Virtual Front Door

A True Story

Bonnie Martin was preparing herself emotionally for widowhood. It was Sunday, August 2, 2015, and Bill, her husband of over 40 years, was going to die. That's not what his doctor said, but it was the truth. Bonnie knew it, and she thought Bill probably knew it, too, though, from the way he was talking and the questions he seemed to make a point of *not* asking, it was pretty clear to her that he wasn't quite ready to accept it yet, even if she was. Ready to accept the *reality of the situation*, that is. What she was not ready to accept, even as she was making her own private preparations, was that it had to happen now. And that's why she was on the Internet: she was looking for information, options, answers, and maybe, just maybe, a little hope . . .

On Cleveland Clinic's website, a little window popped up asking if she would like to "live chat" with a Heart and Vascular Institute nurse. Bonnie decided yes, that was exactly what she wanted to do. During that chat the Cleveland Clinic nurse said something that changed, quite literally, everything, first for her, and eventually for her husband. Even after Bonnie had spent quite a bit of time describing her husband's dire situation, with his many surgeries (including a triple heart bypass) and his extremely complicated medical history—a history that was so complex, in fact, that it had finally caused his doctors at home to say that he was too weak to survive any further interventions, so that all they could do was wait—the Cleveland Clinic nurse typed, "You know, you haven't scared me off yet."

Hello!
Chat with a Cleveland Clinic Heart and Vascular Nurse.

And that, Bonnie remembers, was a very good thing for her to read.

What Bonnie's husband had was an abdominal aortic aneurism, or a "triple A," which meant that, deep inside his body, he had developed a dangerous enlargement in the portion of his aortic artery that extended through his abdomen.[1] The aorta, which is about a foot long and a little more than an inch in diameter,[2] is the human body's largest and most important single artery; it originates at the heart's left ventricle and runs down near the spine into the abdomen, where it splits into the two smaller common iliac arteries.[3] Almost all of Bill's major organs receive their oxygenated blood through his aorta, which also distributes blood to the rest of his body through a process called systemic circulation, which is the constant cycle that pushes oxygen-rich blood out from his heart and returns oxygen-depleted blood back to his lungs.[4] Like most arteries, Bill's aorta is elastic, which allows it to be filled with blood that is under high pressure. Over time, Bill's aorta had developed an aneurysm, which means that a portion of his arterial wall had become weak, distending out like a bubble in a garden hose. Eventually, the pressure generated by the natural circulatory process would push his weakened arterial wall past its limit, and his aneurysm would rupture. Since a ruptured aortic aneurysm can very quickly cause life-threatening internal bleeding, aneurysms are best corrected by an operation before they have a chance to burst.

By the time of Bonnie's online chat with the Cleveland Clinic nurse, Bill had been living with his condition for about 13 years. When it was first discovered, the aneurysm was quite small, allowing his physicians to monitor it over time. It was only when its diameter exceeded five centimeters that it actually became more dangerous not to do something than it was to go ahead and perform a surgical intervention that, depending on the individual patient's circumstances and personal choice, can either be an open surgery or an endo-vascular repair.

In an open procedure, the surgeon makes an incision and removes the abdominal aortic aneurysm, replacing it with a graft section of artery. Open surgical repair is a proven procedure with acceptable risks, but it involves a long recovery period, with an average hospital stay of five to eight days and a return to normal activity in six to 12 weeks. As with any operation, open surgical repair presents the risk of complications.[5]

In an endovascular (which means "inside or within a blood vessel")[6] intervention, a small fabric tube supported from within by tiny metal ribs called a stent graft is intro-duced through incisions made in the groin. The surgeon moves the stent graft up through the arteries that carry blood from the aorta until it is opened directly inside the aneurysm. The stent graft reinforces the weakened part of the vessel from the inside, creating a new channel through which blood can flow, eliminating the risk of rupture. This procedure usually takes one to three hours to perform, and patients generally leave the hospital in one or two days, returning to normal activity in two to six weeks. Again, like all medical procedures, endovascular repair presents a risk of complications; but unlike an open procedure, it also involves regular CT scans and follow-up visits with a physician who uses the scans to help evaluate the status of the stent.[7]

When the time for a decision first arrived, Bill opted for the less invasive endovascular stent. Over the course of the next 13 years, he had 11 more endovascular procedures, including one in January and one in December of 2014. During his recovery from the last procedure he developed anemia from ulcers in his esophagus and stomach, and then polyps were discovered in his colon. Following two colon surgeries in May he was, as Bonnie describes it, "just flattened," so the timing could not have been worse for the news that his triple A had grown to the truly alarming size of 10 centimeters.

As serious as the aneurysm was, Bill's vascular surgeon decided that Bill absolutely had to have some recovery time from his colon surgeries before he would be strong enough to undergo another procedure. But when he met with Bill and Bonnie in July, he discovered that Bill, in his opinion, was still too weak for surgery. His advice, therefore, was that they should wait until the aneurysm ruptured, at which time they would have no choice but to intervene—which Bonnie took to mean that her husband was going to die, since a ruptured aortic aneurysm is a catastrophic occurrence with an extremely high risk of mortality.

As a retired teacher of elementary school music, Bonnie Martin is accustomed to spending a lot of time online. She even maintains several websites, including the Retired Teachers' Association site for her district near Rochester, New York. While there might be a general, if exaggerated stereotype of "older" people not being very computer savvy, Bonnie is quick to point out that it was members of her generation who were among the first to use cell phones and automated teller machines, debit cards and personal computers, e-mail and, yes, even the Internet. Today, she remains fascinated by the Internet, and says of her iPhone, "It's like having the Library of Congress in my hand. The exchange of information that it allows, in medicine, and science, it's just a source of wonder that never gets old for me. So when I needed information about Bill's condition and the places that might be able to help him, I naturally turned to the Internet. And I am really glad I did."

She started her search with some names she knew: Johns Hopkins, Mayo Clinic, Massachusetts General Hospital, New York Presbyterian. Because a family friend had undergone cardiac surgery at Cleveland Clinic and couldn't stop talking about how wonderful his experience had been she eventually found her way to Cleveland Clinic's website. And while it would have been perfectly reasonable for her to have been initially skeptical about the practical value of an online chat, given the seriousness and urgency of her concerns, she remembers that when the nurse chat box popped up onscreen she felt an immediate sense of hope.

"And of course," she recalls, "you hear all the time how important it is to get a second opinion when you have a serious medical issue—so when the nurse chat window appeared on my screen I suddenly realized, 'Hey! We never got a second opinion for Bill.' So as we began to chat, my frame of mind changed. I went from being fearful and almost resigned to wanting . . . to more like *needing* to take some kind of action, to feel as if I could make an impact on what was happening, to exert some control. I think that's what the nurse really did for me—she helped me understand that there were things we could do, and that there was a whole team of doctors and nurses at Cleveland Clinic who were ready to help us do them.

"After the chat," Bonnie says, "I told Bill what the nurse had said about going to Cleveland Clinic for an evaluation. He was still pretty weak, and he doesn't like traveling when he's not feeling well, so we had to wait quite a while before he was strong enough to make the five-hour trip to Cleveland. And since his surgeons at home had been taking care of him for over 13 years, there was also the loyalty issue. But finally, the week before Labor Day, we did it . . . we made the trip; and on the following Tuesday Dr. Kirksey[8] called to discuss Bill's results.

"What he said was that, as far as he could see, there was no reason that Bill wouldn't survive the surgery. In fact, he gave him a 90 percent chance of survival versus a 100 percent chance of death if he didn't have it. He answered all our questions, and I remember at one point he said, 'I just wish I could draw what I'm describing for you.' Then he said, 'Hold on. Are you using a cell phone? What kind is it?' When I told him that we were talking on an iPhone, he said, 'Let's hang up, and I'll call you back with FaceTime.' We did, and as he was explaining everything to us, we watched him draw a picture of what he was going to do on a piece of paper on his desk. Later he scanned that picture and e-mailed it to us. I still have it."

After discussing their new options with their son, Bonnie and Bill decided that it was time to commit. So, on September 25, 2015, Bill underwent a six-hour procedure at Cleveland Clinic to repair his abdominal aortic aneurysm. He spent two days in the intensive care unit before being moved to a step-down unit, and then on October 1, he was transferred to a rehabilitation facility back home in Rochester. Since then, Bonnie reports, his recovery has been progressing slowly, which she says is understandable given all that he's been through.

"Bill's had a lot of surgery in the past couple of years," she says, "and the colon surgeries were especially difficult. But he's getting better every day, so I'm very optimistic, which I can't say was true on the day that I first began searching the Internet. I can truly say that, looking back, Bill's journey back to health started with a pop-up box on Cleveland Clinic's website. That nurse chat was the difference between my husband living or dying. I'm grateful for the website, and for the nurse chat feature. The ability to talk about all of his problems and for her to say, 'It's okay; even if his case is complex, we can still help,' it made all the difference. If the website didn't have that nurse chat feature, it just wouldn't have the same effect. Basically, without that pop-up, I probably would never have taken Bill to Cleveland, and there's a very good chance he would have died from a ruptured aorta. So that's how important that nurse chat was to me personally, and to my family. That website, and that nurse, they made a real difference in our lives."

From Health Information Technology to Healthcare Internet Technology

The story Bonnie Martin tells about her husband Bill's recent healthcare experiences, and how much a "simple" website feature impacted those experiences and their outcome, is the ideal place to begin our health information technology discussion because it is a functional illustration of just how incredibly important technology, technology-based devices, and, most of all, the Internet have become to health information and healthcare-related decisions. In fact, according to a January 2014 Pew Internet Project survey, 87 percent of adults in the United States use the Internet, with 72 percent of those adult users—like Bonnie Martin—searching for health information online during the previous 12 months. Of the people who did an online search for health information, 77 percent used a search engine such as Google, Bing, or Yahoo.[9]

So, as counterintuitive as it may at first appear, the Internet is actually the *only* place our exploration of health information technology's potential transformative capacity can begin because the Internet is, by any realistic measure, the most significant connectivity and communication technology in the history of humankind. Nothing, other than perhaps the invention of language itself, even compares; and there are some aspects of the Internet that are so uniquely human that it is becoming increasingly difficult *not* to see ourselves directly reflected in its design and function—our strengths and faults, our wisdom and foolishness, our wishes and desires, good and bad, positive and negative, constructive and irrationally dyspeptic.

The Internet is, in fact, so vast and complex that, whenever we try to describe what it is and what it does, we are almost inevitably reduced to simply estimating the amount of traffic that moves through it during a specified period of time. And since the physical substance flowing through the Internet is actually a crackling stream of electrons racing from place to place at nearly the speed of light (not unlike the electrochemical nature of the thoughts and physiologic commands zipping around inside our heads and up and down our spines),[10] what we are really trying to measure when we make these volume estimates is the amount of informational work that is being done by all that transmitted electricity. Toward that end, as our descriptive terms of choice, we generally wind up relying on compound words that have *bit* or *byte* as their root.

As we know, computers think in 0s and 1s. A *bit*, which can be either a 0 or a 1 (but not both), is the smallest unit of computer "thought." A *byte* is eight bits, which is just enough storage to capture and record a single alphabetic letter or numerical digit.[11] A gigabyte, or GB, is about a billion bytes, which is the space it takes to hold all the textual information contained in roughly 1,000 books.[12]

With just these three simple notches (a bit, a byte, and a gigabyte) carved into our imaginary measuring stick, we have all the information we need to form at least a general impression of what it means when we say that, in 1992, about 100 GB of digital data moved across the entire Internet every *day*; in 2002, that volume had increased to 100 GB every *second*; and by 2019, it is estimated that at a blistering rate of 51,794 GBs per second,[13] the digital volume equivalent of the textual information contained in almost four and a half *trillion* books will be transmitted across the Internet every 24 hours—or at least it will be until the Internet's speed and total volume capacity increase again, which they almost surely will.

(By the way, as a mental image, if we had a stack of four and a half trillion *dollar bills*, with each bill being .0043 inches thick,[14] our stack would be 305,397 miles tall, meaning that it would stretch past the moon by 66,647 miles. Also, as far as books go, Google Books recently calculated that only about 130 million books have *ever* been written,[15] which is .0029 percent[16] of the four and a half trillion books' worth of information that will be moving through the Internet per day in the not-so-distant future.)

Now obviously it's hard to wrap your head around those kinds of numbers. But that's precisely the point because, in the history of human invention, the Internet is unprecedented in its range of impact, speed of development, and ability to create connections, which, as we are about to see, is by far its most significant capability.[17]

So why is all that true? What is it about the Internet that makes it so widely applicable to the lives of so many people, from so many cultures, living in so many different places across the globe? What does the Internet as a concept and as a physical entity have to do with the potential benefits HIT could deliver as part of the contemporary model of medical practice? And finally, what can we, as members of the

healthcare community and as consumers of healthcare services, do to make sure that we derive the greatest value from
this technology as it presently exists? And what should we
expect from it as it continues to develop in the future?

In the interest of simplicity, the potential answers to these
questions can be summarized in the following three interre-
lated statements:

1. The Internet is the most powerful communication,
   relationship management, and transactional tool
   ever created because it satisfies some of the fundamental social needs of human beings by functioning
   in a way that reflects how we think, work, and interact so accurately that we have not even scratched the
   surface of its potential.

2. To maximize health information technology's transformative power on a truly broad scale, we must
   devise a value equation that places its various component parts into a larger, more meaningful context
   that will encourage the financial investment and
   commitment of time and energy necessary to connect every provider and every patient in a new kind
   of technology-enabled medical practice space.

3. To the practice of medicine HIT has the potential
   to be what the Internet is to human communication and social interaction *if* a universal browser-like
   interface between people and machines can connect
   us to an "Internet of Healthcare" that is so secure,
   accessible, and easy to use that it becomes an ever-
   present extension of our healthcare-related thoughts,
   actions, and activities.

Hopefully, by concentrating on these three ideas, this
discussion will help emphasize how important it is that HIT

and its associated functions move more directly into clinical practice, which is where it must go. And the sooner the better, because for a technical function to become a really effective clinical tool, it must be owned, as much as possible, by the people who actually use it. For that to happen, traditional organizational models, especially those related to the rigid, hierarchical "org chart" structure of most IT departments, will have to change in some pretty radical ways.

First, clinicians will need to tolerate, and then expect active participation by their IT colleagues in clinical practice in ways that will require admitting a series of new faces into what was formerly the sacrosanct territory of the white coat and stethoscope. IT professionals will need to take responsibility for freeing themselves of the technical jargon that often serves as password protection for their own exclusive society so that they and their clinical partners will not only communicate better, but begin collaborating at a level that neither ever imagined possible (or even necessary). And we all—clinicians, IT professionals, payors, and patients—will need to understand that the ways things were done in the past are just not good enough today, and that once it is truly transformed from what some have called "sick care,"[18] healthcare will no longer be confined to a doctor's examination or operating room, becoming instead an integral part of a healthier, more proactively positive way of life.

Before we begin our examination of what HIT can be, let's establish a little context by taking a closer (albeit very brief) look at each of our three concept statements, beginning with how the Internet can be seen as a place where hundreds of years of technical development and thousands of years of basic human nature come together in a confluence that points the way directly toward healthcare's future.

Does that sound like a bit of a stretch?

Well, to understand where we're going, we should first understand where we've been, because, when it comes to the Internet and HIT, the more we know about the technology involved, the more we will find ourselves focusing on the *people* we use it to serve.

We Have Met the Internet, and It Is Us

The explosion that started driving personal computers and the Internet directly into just about every corner of our daily lives started sometime between 1995 and 2000—which is not to say that before then computers were a novel or exotic concept in the public's consciousness. Famously, the team at Bletchley Park in England constructed a kind of early computer to help them crack Nazi codes, including the "unbreakable" Enigma cipher used to control the deadly "wolf pack" submarines patrolling the North Atlantic during World War II.[19] NASA used computers that were less powerful than the average pocket calculator to put a man on the moon.[20] And Steven King had been writing his bestsellers on a Wang word processor since the mid-1980s.[21] But something happened right around Y2K (remember the Y2K bug?), and once it did, it felt like computers and the Internet turned a corner and never looked back.

The evolutionary trajectories of our society and of the machines we make intersected right at the moment when we finally taught those machines to effectively "talk" to one another in a way that was *simple* enough for the average, non–computer-science–trained person to understand, and yet *flexible* enough to allow a whole lot of people to do a multitude of things. The reason that the result—the World Wide Web, or the Internet—proved to be such a game changer, is that suddenly an entire globally distributed network of enormously fast computational machines stopped working in

FIGURE 1.1 Connectivity/Relationship Network Timelines

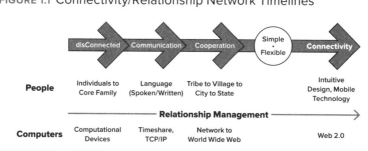

isolation from one another, becoming part of a coordinated structure that directly reflects how we take in information, access and process what we know, organize ourselves into groups, and communicate and work with others. As a consequence, the Internet changed the way we live our lives forever.

A simplified version of the parallel paths that we humans and our machines followed, from self-contained, self-sufficient individuals to connected participants in an ever-expanding, increasingly complex network of relationships, is shown in Figure 1.1. And while there are many interesting aspects of the complementary histories of humans and our machines, there are two shared features of these histories that hold special significance. The first, as we have already briefly mentioned, is how critical the dual "simple/flexible" concept is to the success of even the most complex activities (which, for the Internet, finds its ultimate culmination in the universal browser); and the second is what might be called the fractal nature of the human journey.

A fractal is an object that displays a self-similarity, meaning that its component parts have the same mathematical characteristics as the whole.[22] Part of what makes fractals so fascinating is how deeply fundamental they are to the way the world is organized. All around us we can see simple structures

FIGURE 1.2 Simple Fractal

that can be built into amazingly complex shapes that can then themselves become part of even more complex and intricate structures (Figure 1.2), such as the classic Fibonacci sequence, a numeric series in which each successive number is the sum of the two numbers that preceded it (1, 1, 2, 3, 5, 8, 13, etc.).[23]

When drawn, the Fibonacci sequence renders the elegant "golden spiral"[24] (Figure 1.3), which is reminiscent of so many shapes in nature (such as the beautiful shell of the nautilus mollusk, or the vortex patterns of swirling water).

One way the fractal quality of the history of human society can be seen is in the way our basic interpersonal/social structures, from family to clan, clan to band, band to tribe, tribe to village, village to city, city to city state, etc.[25] seem to repurpose the same basic relationship constructs in progressively larger and more complex social networks, which are themselves self-regulated by size because of our innate human ability to effectively manage only up to a maximum number of personal relationships (as observed by Robin Dunbar, an anthropologist and psychologist at the University of Oxford).

Based on the social brain hypothesis,[26] which postulates that primates need big brains because they live in complex social organizations, Dunbar calculated the number of

FIGURE 1.3 Golden Spiral

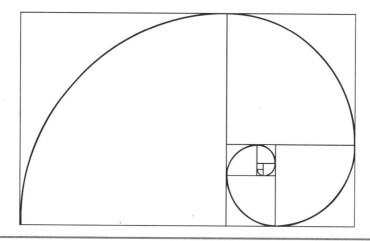

people with whom one individual human being can maintain a reasonably meaningful relationship at about 150.[27] Beyond 150, relationships become increasingly confused and unmanageable. From U.S. Marine fighting units to Amish and Mennonite sects that always split when they reach a certain number of members, there are dozens of examples of how human social groups self-regulate according to size.

But before we could even imagine entering into anything beyond the most basic of social relationships, people needed a way to communicate the fact that they were ready and willing to cooperate, and that's where language comes in. It has been suggested that human beings began using some kind of language as far back as 60,000 years ago,[28] and it was this amazing technology that, some believe, helped start humanity's migration out of Africa and into Europe, Asia, and beyond. In an interesting parallel with the developmental history of computers, written language is thought to have begun not as a way to capture abstract thoughts but instead as a way to count important things, such as the amount of grain a farmer had to trade—so the first written language may actually have been numbers.[29]

Numbers are important to language in another way, because the number of hours it takes to learn a language may be a factor in how likely people are to choose to use it. For example, the average number of hours it takes an English speaker to learn Spanish, which shares many of English's grammatical rules and constructs, is about 600, or approximately 24 weeks.[30] Comparatively, it takes an English speaker an average of 2,200 hours, or 88 weeks, to learn Mandarin Chinese,[31] which has approximately 4,000 characters required for functional literacy.[32] This observation is not intended as a comment on the inherent qualities or utility of any language, and when we combine its eight most common variations, Chinese is the most spoken language on the planet.[33] But the comparative ease with which English can be learned, at least to a state of transactional proficiency, by native speakers of many different languages, along with its increased utility as its sheer number of speakers increase, are likely contributing factors in its ranking as the most common *second* language in the world.[34]

So now that we've boiled down most of human history to an ongoing exercise in adapting a basic core relationship model to social structures of increasing complexity while always searching for the simplest way to say and do things, let's take a look at how the history of computers and the Internet followed pretty much this same path.

The Power of Networking

Depending on how far we want to stretch the concept, the first mechanical "computer" was probably the abacus, which made its debut in ancient Babylonia in about 2,400 BCE.[35] Leonardo da Vinci noodled around with an idea for a mechanical calculating machine in his sixteenth-century notebooks,[36] and early analog computers were integral to the development of the atomic bomb at Los Alamos.[37] But the first computer that really established a sense of itself in the public's imagination is probably the Universal Automatic Computer, or UNIVAC, which became a "modern magic brain"[38] due, in large part, to the famous picture of Harry S. Truman holding up a copy of the *Chicago Tribune* that bore the headline, "Dewey Defeats Truman."

In the picture, an obviously pleased president displays a headline that incorrectly announces his loss to Republican challenger Thomas E. Dewey, governor of New York. The date was November 3, 1948,[39] and four years *later*, when the Columbia Broadcasting System (CBS) failed to predict the outcome of the presidential race between retired army general Dwight D. Eisenhower and Adlai Stevenson, Democratic governor of Illinois, even though they had an accurate projection in hand, that photograph of President Truman holding his souvenir newspaper would help make the UNIVAC the most famous computer on earth.

UNIVAC 1 was an eight-ton behemoth that was developed by a division of Remington Rand.[40] It was as big as a one-car garage, had thousands of vacuum tubes that processed about 10,000 operations per second (compared to today's supercomputers that are measured in quadrillions of operations per second), and cost about $1 million ($8 million in contemporary cash). Traditional pre-election polling had established an expectation that the Eisenhower/Stevenson race would be a close one, so when UNIVAC spit out its pronouncement of an easy Eisenhower victory, CBS, with the Truman/Dewey goof still fresh in the media's collective mind, decided to err on the side of caution by not broadcasting the projection.[41] Later that night, when the final tabulations showed that UNIVAC's prediction was in fact less than one percentage point off, CBS confessed that the computer had been right all along.[42] This is pretty much where the image of the computer as an all-knowing, card-spitting, lightbulb-blinking piece of mechanical wizardry likely got its start. It is also more or less where public perception stayed throughout the sixties, seventies and even into the early eighties. Computers were autonomous, self-contained, big, and inscrutable. They could even be calmly menacing, like the utterly detached HAL 9000 mega-computer in Stanley Kubrick's science fiction epic *2001: A Space Odyssey*.[43] HAL stood for Heuristically (capable of learning or discovering for oneself)[44] programmed ALgorithmic (a set of instructions for solving a problem)[45] computer. It made such an impression that it wasn't until the 1990s that most people stopped seeing computers as isolated, big brain machines and started thinking of them more as the component pieces in an enormous, connected global network.[46]

It was at that point—when computers began connecting with one another in fact, and in the popular imagination—that they, like human society itself, began advancing toward an entirely different level of success. Also like humans, before computers could begin working together in increasingly large and more complex networks, they needed a language of their own, which came in two parts.

The first emerged from the U.S. Pentagon's Advanced Research Projects Agency Network, or ARPANET, which was an initiative that allowed for computer "time-sharing" between several academic and research organizations that were doing work for the Department of Defense. Called the Transfer Control Protocol (TCP) or, more simply, the Internet Protocol (IP),[47] this breakthrough nomenclature system made it possible for different kinds of computers in different locations to "talk" to one another by specifying the format of addresses and units of transmission.

The second part of the language that enabled connected computing started in 1991 when Tim Berners-Lee, a

London-born physicist working at CERN (Conseil Européen pour la Recherche Nucléaire), the European laboratory for particle physics in Geneva, Switzerland, made the source code of a project he spearheaded called WWW, or the World Wide Web, available to the public.[48] Originally begun as a way to organize the information contained in multiple databases across different locations in CERN's network, which at the time was the largest in Europe, WWW has been called the world's first Internet browser because it made it possible for information to be "tagged" as "hypertext," and for "websites," which at the time were simply text-based documents, to be "bookmarked" so they could be located again when needed.[49]

Even with this new language in place, the real Internet, the one that we would recognize as the vehicle we use to check our online bank statements, order items through Amazon, connect with our friends on Facebook, or simply read the latest news on our favorite smartphone app, didn't take off until the two-sided "simple/flexible" variable represented in Figure 1.1 made interacting with a computer feel less like completing an electric green slow-motion math quiz and more like a direct extension of our hands and thoughts. For that to happen, the clunky, text-only, computer scientist line-of-code method of typing cryptic backslash–backslash–Function Key–ENTER commands, which was the mainstay of the Internet's early days, had to go away—which it did when computers got GUI.

It's Pronounced "Gooey," and It Made Computers Sticky

The idea of the graphical user interface, or GUI, a methodology that allows users to interact with electronic devices through icons instead of text-based commands,[50] is said to stretch back to the early radar displays of the 1940s and

1950s.[51] In the 1960s, scientists at the Augmentation Research Center in California first developed the oNLine System, which was a computer program with a display that featured a cursor, multiple "windows," and a point-and-click style mouse, all based on the hand-eye coordination development process seen in the early learning patterns of young children.[52] In 1984, Apple introduced the Macintosh, which became the first commercially successful computer with a multiwindow interface, files that looked like sheets of paper, file directories that were shaped like file folders, and graphic representations of real-world desktop accessories such as a calculator.[53] It was also the first computer to have a trashcan icon on its screen for deleting files that were no longer useful. In 1985, Microsoft released Windows 1.0, though it wasn't until the launch of Windows 3.0 in 1990 that the market really started taking off.[54]

In 1993 inventor Marc Andreessen released Mosaic, which is often called the world's first truly popular, user-friendly browser.[55] By applying GUI concepts to how people could interact with the Internet, Andreessen started the evolving Internet down a path that led directly to where we are today: an Internet that is so inherently useful and that still has so much potential yet to be realized that it makes the uplifting story of Bonnie and Bill Martin possible. Suddenly, with the introduction of a system that made intuitive sense to users, the mysteries of what was "inside" the Internet began to fade, and web browsing, or surfing, began.

For many of us, this was an exciting period of real discovery, when an entirely new space, called *cyberspace* after a term first coined by science fiction writer William Gibson in his 1982 story "Burning Chrome,"[56] began to feel like a "real" space, where "real" things seemed to be happening. It was during this period, right around 1996, that a Cleveland Clinic colleague memorably called the Internet a "time machine" because she would find herself so absorbed by it that, when she finally blinked her way back to reality, she would discover that those few minutes she thought she had spent online were actually hours she had lost to the siren song of cyberspace.

Following Mosaic's initial success, Andreessen founded his own company, Netscape, which, in 1994, produced the popular, paradigm-changing Netscape Navigator.[57] Soon thereafter, in 1995, Microsoft introduced Internet Explorer,[58] and the "browser wars"[59] were officially on. Today, through popular browsers such as Explorer, Firefox, Edge, Opera, Chrome, and Safari,[60] the Internet is so easy to use that even those with little or no formal training have so thoroughly integrated it into both the workplace and the home-space that, for many, it's hard to imagine a time when it was not a part of everyday life.

Some of the effects of this transition toward intuitive usability are truly amazing. For example, a recent survey released by Kleiner, Perkins, Caufield & Byers tells us that, in 2014, the average adult in the United States spent 444 minutes, or seven hours and 24 minutes, of every day looking at a screen.[61] The numbers were similar in the United Kingdom (six hours, 51 minutes), Canada (six hours, 16 minutes), and Germany (six hours, 19 minutes). Computer technology, in the form of handheld devices, has also become so ergonomically streamlined that many of the most popular phones and tablets have only one or two of what we might describe as buttons anywhere on them. A recent Baylor University study suggests that smartphones are just as addictive as drugs or alcohol.[62] And now, according to many leading voices in the increasingly intimate space where technology and commerce coalesce, even GUI may be more of a burden than users are willing to endure. Enter voice interfaces, or VI, through which we will soon simply talk to our machines, and our machines will talk back.[63]

Healthcare Internet Technology: A Value Equation for Healthcare's "Browser"

So how does all of this impact healthcare? In a word, positively. The time has passed when clinicians and administrative professionals need to know much, if anything, about the technical components that make the Internet (or, indeed, much of the technology that is delivered through their own internal networks) work. The Internet is now a worldwide infrastructure, so big and multilayered that it can't really be described as a single "thing" at all. It is a growing global utility, and the emerging Internet2, a blazingly fast, presently private improvement over what is now being called Internet1, will, once a business model is developed through which it can be made available to users beyond its present cohort of academic universities, select private companies, and governmental agencies, doubtlessly move the needle yet again.[64]

But the crucial concept to understand about the resource we call the Internet is the power and transformative impact of the browser, because it is the browser that made the Internet a single, predictable experience. In addition to connecting a whole bunch of different machines that do an enormous number of different things, the browser put a face to Internet-based activities that human beings can understand and manage. It is the browser's core function of translating information from multiple sources into a coherent, actionable experience (which expands the concept beyond those systems that we have come to call "search engines") that is represented by Figure 1's "simple/flexible" circle.

For example: one common task most of us in the traveling public regularly conduct online is searching for and purchasing airline tickets. Through sites such as Expedia or Orbitz, travelers can log in, type in their city of origin, their destination, and their desired trip times and dates, and the site scours the Internet for options that meet these criteria. Every airline has its own Internet-based scheduling and payment system, and they are all different—they look different, and they behave differently. But these single, user-friendly travel-support sites serve to translate everything they can find that matches the user's parameters, anywhere on the Internet, in a single, manageable way that allows travelers to pick the right option for the right price and, with the click of a mouse, pay for and book their flight.

That is the power of the browser, the single "simple/flexible" breakthrough that ignited the Internet's amazingly rapid growth and adoption, the interface point that connects two different, though similar, processing systems: the human brain and the microchip. You, as the user, do not have to understand anything other than how to use the travel site of your choice because the site, working within the infrastructure of the various target sites it identifies, does all the "background" work, connecting you to only the information you need to accomplish your task in a way that streamlines your portion of the transaction.

If we apply that same paradigm to what we call health information technology, or HIT, today, reimagining HIT as healthcare Internet technology, we can now see that, to navigate the rapidly expanding cyberspace of clinical care, the common "browser" of medical practice must be based on the electronic medical record (EMR), or, more accurately, since it directly involves the patient in the healthcare equation in ways that were previously not possible, the EHR, or electronic *health* record. By integrating all the various systems clinicians and patients need according to design standards that allow them to function in a truly interoperable way, the EHR can become, like a browser on the broader Internet, healthcare's primary enabling function (and even, ultimately, its real-language-driven decision-support function).

This same perspective, from which we see HIT as the enabling infrastructure for all the processes and tasks associated with delivering healthcare—from real-time decision support at the bedside that is "smart" enough to synthesize the entirety of our existing medical literature into something so comprehensible that it becomes an active part of every clinician's thought process, to mobile health and wellness programs that utilize handheld devices, such as smartphones, and wearable devices, such as Fitbits, to help users engage in healthier, more wellness-conscious lifestyles—will also help us change the way we think about how we account for the cost of these systems on a balance sheet. Because it is an unfortunate, if predictable, reality that, during the past decade or so, the emerging concept of HIT has become a blanket term for pretty much any computer-based system that does just about anything even vaguely related to healthcare.

This lack of definition creates so much opportunity for Rorschach-like interpretations that it can be difficult to explain exactly what HIT is—though it never seems hard to say what it costs, which is always "a lot." And with federal regulators, public and private payors, and patients all demanding unprecedented levels of clarity around the purchasing power of every dollar they spend, a detailed understanding of HIT's true value has never been more important. But how do you measure something that you can't yet define?

The simple answer is, you don't. If we are ever going to truly understand what HIT costs compared to the value it actually delivers for payors, clinicians, and patients alike, we are going to have to do two things:

1. Define it.

2. Formulate a workable value equation that will begin to accurately capture the amount of real benefit it can be expected to deliver.

FIGURE 1.4 Healthcare Internet Technology (HIT) Value Equation

$$\text{Value} = \frac{\text{Integrated Services}}{\text{Cost}}$$

One excellent starting point in our effort to imagine HIT's true value equation might be the famous formula put forth by renowned authors, researchers, and lecturers Michael Porter and Elizabeth Teisberg, in which they measure healthcare's value as health outcomes achieved per dollar spent.[65] This same idea is often rendered as Value = Quality ÷ Cost; with additional versions featuring refinements such as defining Quality as "Outcomes, Safety, and Service,"[66] or adding the concept of "Functional Value" in which Value = (Performance + Capability) ÷ Cost = Function/Cost.[67]

The very simple equation represented in Figure 1.4 is one way to imagine a healthcare Internet technology value equation in which HIT is described not as a single system or service (like UNIVAC or the other isolated, individually functioning computers) but as a series of interoperable IT-enabled solutions to an entire range of clinical and business needs that, taken together, not only deliver value but actually make the contemporary model of medical practice possible.

Just as an Internet browser works to translate all the electrically charged information blazing through cyberspace into an intuitively useable experience, the integrated EHR, or electronic health record, has the potential to become the "browser" that will make a future of HIT, or healthcare Internet technology–based innovation possible in the emerging cyber-care health space.

By removing the impression that it is somehow beneficial for provider organizations to attempt to account for a measurable return on investment (ROI) for each system that enables its e-mail, EHR, image management, and other clinical and administrative functions *individually*, we must begin creating a HIT value equation that will more accurately describe how an integrated HIT system *as a functional whole* actually impacts a provider organization's ability to manage and deliver all the different aspects of quality care in an increasingly competitive market. Because it is only when we step back and see our operations from a more elevated perspective (that is itself enabled by the data access and analytics capabilities HIT can deliver) that we realize that the dividing lines between clinical operations and "IT support" are blurring so much that they will soon cease to exist at all.

As we will see in our review of some of Cleveland Clinic's day-to-day operations that follow, there is almost nothing that IT cannot impact. From the employee identification system that automatically lifts the gate once it verifies that the sticker on the windshield of an employee's car is correct for a particular garage or parking lot, to the wand a surgical nurse specialist uses to scan every single bar-coded item used during an open-heart surgery directly into an automated medical supply management system, to the digital pedometer members of our employee health plan use to keep track of the steps they take over the course of the day as part of Cleveland Clinic's "Healthy Choices" wellness program, the integrated healthcare Internet technology system we are building for our organization is an active component in the way we care for our patients and ourselves. It is even helping inform our strategic plans for the future growth of our national and international operation.

Going Forward

Building on this conceptual framework, let's begin our tour of Cleveland Clinic's HIT-enabled practice model, starting with the outward-facing public persona represented on our Internet pages and their rapidly expanding complement of specialized social media locations. As we are about to see, no one is more immediately or directly affected by the dynamics of the Internet than our Marketing and Interactive Web Services teams, and no one better embodies the attitude that we believe we all must embrace when it comes to understanding the Internet as a healthcare tool, which is that, instead of spending our time wondering how it works, we should be imaging what else it can do.

SUMMARY

1. The Internet is a valid, analogous model for the developmental path of all complex technology-based solutions because it demonstrates how isolated, individualized systems and functions exponentially increased in effectiveness and utility only after they became part of a larger, integrated technology system that was easy to access and easy to use. The way the Internet moved from a specialized, niche system owned and operated by individuals and organizations with specialized technology interests and experience to an intuitive tool embraced by the general population presages the potential of integrated information technology systems in medical practice if the core usability requirements of simplicity and flexibility can be met for a critical mass of professional and other users.

2. The healthcare Internet technology value statement of Value = Integrated Services ÷ Cost is meant to illustrate that, when viewed as a technical ecosystem instead of as a series of isolated, problem-focused solutions, interoperable HIT systems are actually the ubiquitous connectivity building blocks from which the contemporary medical practice model will be fabricated. The real value of these technologies is the integrated system they enable, which cannot be accurately represented by measuring the cost of the individual parts of which the overall system is composed.

3. HIT systems, like the amalgam of different machines and software algorithms that taken together we call the Internet, will experience a truly profound increase in adoption and use across the entire healthcare space only when they are able to connect all clinical care providers, administrative users, and patients to all the information and services they need, regardless of source or location, through a universal browser-like EHR experience.

Bottom Line

Though we may often talk about technology as if it is somehow a force that is separate from us and that has its own unique attributes, awareness, and even its own agenda, our technology is, in fact, an extension of our imaginations, minds, and hands. Our technology is not a separate "thing," it is a direct extension of the people who create, use, and improve it.

Chapter 2

Vertical Thinking in the Mouse Museum

The web page through which Bonnie Martin first connected to a Cleveland Clinic Heart and Vascular Institute nurse is just one part of a much larger "digital ecosystem" of coordinated static and dynamic content, interactive clinical and administrative services, and established and emerging social media platforms that took multiple teams of medical, operational, marketing, and IT professionals literally decades to design and build. It is the product of years of experience and experimentation; it features some of the most popular and respected online health information content in the world; and the one single fixed and constant thing about it is that it is always in motion. Always. It literally never stops changing. Ever. It can't, because if it did, it would immediately recede into the rearview mirror of online relevancy because right now, even as you read these words, the critical mass of all those wildly popular technology-based consumer products absolutely everyone in the world seems to either have or want is focusing personal communication, retail purchasing, and a myriad of other connectivity and transactional experiences into one single hotspot location: the palm of your hand.

Today, consumer computing is all about going mobile, to the point that augmenting the digital potential of the approximately three billion existing users who are active on the Internet worldwide, the generally accepted 71 percent total penetration of mobile devices that is anticipated to occur by 2019[1] will almost certainly result in a corresponding explosion in demand-driven innovation. With 192 countries, representing nearly half of the world's population, already connected by 3G mobile networks, it won't be long before smartphones and tablets begin outselling PCs,[2] making mobile connectivity the common town square wherein virtually the entirety of humankind will come together to trade, work, and play.

In this new reality of digital mobility, the traditional desktop computer's standard rectangular 1280 by 1024 pixel display configuration, or even the newer 1920 by 1200 pixel landscape orientation of flat-screen monitors, will soon be, if not entirely obsolete, at the very least relegated to second-class status by website designers and content creators as they imagine new and better ways to connect to their rapidly expanding, increasingly sophisticated customer base. Today's designers, including the ones responsible for keeping Cleveland Clinic's web presence on the leading edge of the industry's creativity curve, spend most of their time thinking about how their sites will look in the mobile device vertical. And with the touch screen as the world's emerging navigational interface of choice, drop-down menus and the traditional computer mouse will become a thing of the past.

But there is a distinct difference between exploring visionary possibilities and simply riding a fad. The trick, of course, is knowing (in the moment) which is which; and the stakes, particularly in healthcare, have never been higher. Even if most early Internet adopters originally regarded their websites as—essentially—a compact form of billboard advertising, contemporary attitudes about the potential and purpose of the Internet have evolved into a new kind of online aesthetic called responsive design.[3] By placing the needs and comfort of the user squarely in the center of every decision, responsive design makes easy reading, streamlined navigation, less scrolling, panning, or page resizing, and uniform content deliverability across a range of different devices without the loss of either the visual brand or the integrity of the experience the fundamental guiding commandments of success.

Which is a fancy way of saying that, when it comes to the Internet, experience teaches us to make it fast, make it simple, keep it fresh, and always make sure that everything you do accurately reflects who you are as an organization. Because in the twenty-first century, a website, in a lot of ways, *is* your organization. It is often a prospective patient's (or customer's) first experience of your organization, so it has to represent it well. It has to reflect your values, personality, and sense of purpose. It has to communicate not only the accurate facts and figures related to your organization's performance and product, it has to say something about the spirit of the place. To do that, it has to capture something essential about the people it represents. It also has to offer some opportunity to initiate and conduct actual interactions that deliver some measure of value (for example, there are now real, clinical activities that a patient can initiate through Cleveland Clinic's website that deliver tangible medical services, such as a specialty-specific second medical opinion, that are entirely web-based and that do not require the patient to ever set foot inside one of our physical locations). Additionally, the relentless demand of today's technology-supported marketplace for ever more content that is always new, new, new means that you have to build your web presence on a platform that is so easy to maintain that it won't take a battalion of rocket scientists to keep it fresh.

Finally, but crucially, you must never, not for a moment, lose sight of just how much your exterior, public-facing web pages, combined with the interior-facing intranet components you create for the use of your clinical and administrative employees, will impact how your staff views your organization and their place in it—potentially affecting the sense of engagement and connection they share and, ultimately, the satisfaction of your patients.

How exactly do you do all that? What's the formula or recipe you can follow? Where is the link you can just click to make it all happen?

Not surprisingly, there is no single, "one size fits all" guide to designing and managing a cohesive digital presence—along with its requisite network-based supporting technology tool set—that will fit the unique needs of every organization. The process involves real effort, disciplined thinking, and a substantial commitment to bringing people from every area of your enterprise together for what is essentially a voluntary round of "organizational psychotherapy." The good news is that the outcome will be well worth the time and effort. The better news is that the things you will learn about your organization during the course of transforming it through a more fully integrated technology infrastructure and service set are almost certain to exceed even your most optimistic expectations. When it comes to the potential impact technology can have on a healthcare organization, or indeed, any commercial enterprise, the transformation begins the moment you start thinking about it.

Observing an Effect

In physics, the "observer effect" describes a phenomenon in which the act of looking at something alters, in some way, the thing being observed.[4] Perhaps the simplest example of the observer effect is measuring your tire pressure, since it is next to impossible to use a tire gauge without letting at least a little air out when you do it, making the pressure you measure, by definition, different than it was when you initiated your observation. There are other, increasingly complicated iterations of the observer effect that culminate in the one used in quantum physics, which states that once you have measured a system, that system's current state becomes defined, which stops it from being in any of its other possible states.[5] In other words, measuring or observing a system with an eye to defining its current state opens that system up to the possibility of *becoming* something other than the state we defined.

Sketching out a current state is step one in envisioning the potential universe of future states that we could create if we simply identify our organization's strategic goals and aspirations, line them up next to our present circumstance, and draw circles around the gaps that exist between the two. That's called a gap analysis,[6] and it's the foundational exercise IT professionals traditionally conduct when planning a project or initiative. It's a time-tested process that almost inevitably points toward progress, and it is one of the most valuable exercises you can conduct for the health and future of your business.

At Cleveland Clinic, this process occurred and reoccurred with increasing degrees of buy-in and participation over a 15-year period in which our operating model, technology infrastructure, and digital ecosystem triangulated at a single point of organizational culture that we came to call One Cleveland Clinic. The process required what was, by any definition, an extended period of time principally because there were very few, if any, other healthcare organizations that had conducted similar work at a comparable scale that we could look to for precedent, and also because the iterative outcomes of each progressive step influenced not only the analytical process itself but also the scope of what we came to believe was possible on a much greater perceptual and functional scale. It was not until we had fully committed to this exercise, which was first initiated as a process of identifying the "gaps" in our organizational composition that could be closed through technology, that we began to truly understand exactly what the concept of "One Cleveland Clinic" could really mean. It was during the process of becoming "One Cleveland Clinic" that we all became "caregivers."

So How Many Were There Before?

For anyone unfamiliar with the inner workings of Cleveland Clinic as an organization, appreciating the magnitude of the changes that have happened to our culture and operations over the past decade and a half might be something of a challenge. As counterintuitive as it might appear, much of the initial confusion our employees experienced about this initiative started with the phrase we had originally hoped would provide immediate and unambiguous clarity as to our intent and direction: One Cleveland Clinic.

"Really?" you might well ask. "One Cleveland Clinic? So, how many were there before?"

Even now, after years of increasingly focused work, there still isn't a single, satisfying answer to that question, probably because, when it comes to history, real clarity tends to emerge only well after an event actually occurs. Opportunities and growth, challenges and change all add up to an organic process of continuing evolution that can sometimes lead an organization down some pretty interesting paths and through some potentially complicated tunnels. In Cleveland Clinic's case, the process of growing, in both patient volume and simple physical size, was, in many ways, a process of growing apart, which wasn't anyone's conscious intent, but it was definitely a result. There was a period of time in the late 1990s that the organization had two separate brand identities: one for the Cleveland Clinic main campus and family health centers and another for Cleveland Clinic's system of what was then seven regional hospitals.[7]

Originally founded in 1921 by four physicians who had developed an appreciation for a multidisciplinary approach to medical practice when they served together in World War I, Cleveland Clinic started life as an outpatient clinic, located in a four-story building on what was then, and in many ways still is, Cleveland's main thoroughfare, Euclid Avenue. From the late 1800s through the early 1920s, Euclid Avenue was known as Millionaires' Row.[8]

It was on this stretch of premier Cleveland real estate, populated by some of America's most ardent advocates of unfettered market capitalism, that Cleveland Clinic, a multi-disciplinary group practice organized in a way that reminded some at the time of a kind of communal medical collective, opened for business, right at the tail end of the nation's first "Red Scare," which happened between 1919 and 1920.[9] Following both the entanglements of World War I and the Bolshevik Revolution that saw Czar Nicholas Romanov and his entire family executed in July 1918[10] amid a campaign of mass killing and systematic oppression that came to be known as the Red Terror, a wave of anti-immigrant, anticommunist fervor consumed much of America's political and cultural discourse. Which is a nice way of saying that anything that could be interpreted as even vaguely "un-American" was viewed with, at a minimum, a cold stare of hostile suspicion. So, from day one, because it was "different," Cleveland Clinic had to prove itself—which it did, for generations.

Today, Cleveland Clinic is an integrated regional health-care delivery system with national and international reach. Its 160-acre main campus, located not far from Cleveland's

University Circle, has 44 buildings, which house more than 100 operating rooms, seven hybrid surgical suites, specialized intensive care units (ICUs), research laboratories, pathology laboratories, classrooms, and other facilities. Beyond the main campus, there are 18 full-service family health centers, 9 regional hospitals, plus medical office buildings, all adding up to more than 100 patient care delivery sites in Northeast Ohio alone. In addition to its northern Ohio locations, there is Cleveland Clinic Florida, which includes a hospital and clinic in Weston, and offices in West Palm Beach and, soon, Coral Gables. In Las Vegas, Nevada, we operate the Cleveland Clinic Lou Ruvo Center for Brain Health, where we provide neurological and urological services. Cleveland Clinic Canada, in Toronto, offers a variety of health and wellness services, including sports health and executive health. In the summer of 2015, we opened Cleveland Clinic Abu Dhabi, a project of Mubadala Development Corporation, with more than 300 hospital beds, offering specialty services in heart and vascular disease, digestive disease, eye care, neurology, respiratory, and other areas.

During all this growth and activity, the operational realities of managing an organization this big and this complex meant that just keeping our collaborative physical workflows up and running was a major logistical challenge—especially since the digital connectivity systems that were evolving over the same stretch of time were almost invariably of limited power, prohibitively expensive, and maddeningly slow and unreliable. From its founding in 1921 through 2000, when we first began implementing an electronic medical record system that would be used in all of our facilities, the foundation of Cleveland Clinic's caregiver coordination was, like the rest of the medical world, the same basic paper chart that doctors have been using for over a century—which speaks, in part, to one obvious factor that limits any healthcare organization's ability to sustain growth as an integrated system: simple physical proximity.

When the entirety of Cleveland Clinic was located in one or two buildings, rapidly delivering patient charts to physicians' offices was a fairly simple, if labor-intensive, process of moving reams of paper back and forth between the records "barn" and the examination space. As the organization increased its physical footprint, the process of moving charts required the addition of some technology, which came in the form of carts—first, carts that were pushed along like grocery baskets, and then big electric, motor-powered metal boxes that were maneuvered by a driver standing on a fold-down step.

As new facilities joined the system, each hospital and ambulatory location established its own chart storage and delivery model. But that design could only be stretched so far. When patients were referred by one Cleveland Clinic physician in one location to another Cleveland Clinic physician in another, they quite reasonably expected to be known by the staff when they arrived, which, in practice, was rarely the case. It's extremely hard to move thousands of paper charts back and forth across town every day, on demand.

In some ways, the sense of disconnection patients and caregivers experienced when they moved within the Cleveland Clinic Health System was deliberately designed. Through the 1980s and 1990s, as local hospitals joined the system, the prevailing philosophy was to maintain each facility's "neighborhood flavor" while providing, when necessary, a convenient connection to the highly specialized service set downtown. While a number of progressive leadership voices extolled the potential virtues of a more integrated approach to health system management, the reality was that there just wasn't any practical way to implement the kind of administrative processes that would fundamentally move the health system closer to a single, functional organization from the fairly loose collection of aligned though essentially independent facilities it remained all the way up to the turn of the twenty-first century. In this light, the paper-based medical model can be seen as not only a concession to contemporary realities but as an object illustration of a workflow that was essentially at odds with the organization's underlying multidisciplinary medical mission.

So when, in 2005, Dr. Cosgrove began floating the idea of reimagining the existing health system as a much more cohesive, more standardized Cleveland Clinic provider *organism*, the real question was not if it was a good idea, but how we could make it work. In addition to the basic human interactive challenges that confronted our caregivers as they physically moved from place to place in the organization, such as questions regarding operating procedures or job-related etiquette, there were financial and potential patient safety–related issues that were the direct result of the lack of a set of overall health system operating standards. For example, between the 11 hospitals that made up the health system at the time, 23 different brands and versions of portable ventilators were being used. A respiratory technician filling in on a shift at a hospital just a few miles from his or her primary location could not confidently say that he or she would know how to use this critical piece of equipment.

Now extrapolate that level of variability to include the placement of instruments on a crash cart, inventory and ordering procedures, on-call staffing expectations, paging protocols, and all the other operational and interpersonal understandings that make a hospital efficient and effective, and the challenge of organizing and managing change on such a scale quickly becomes all but incomprehensible. Where would we even start? Which brings us back to IT, and the biggest gap analysis you can possibly imagine.

We're Gonna Need a Bigger Box

The intent of our "observer effect" discussion was to introduce the idea that actually sitting down and looking at your work, how you do it, how you organize it, how you decide if you're doing it well, and how you figure out ways to do it better can be a remarkably beneficial activity. Even in healthcare, with our industry's near obsession with "continuous improvement" programs and "quality metrics," the kinds of fundamentally introspective exercises that force us to dig into the "whys" and "why nots" of our processes and workflows are often hard to do well, especially because care delivery never really stops, or even slows down, particularly in the inpatient setting. But the One Cleveland Clinic initiative, by its very nature, could not be achieved in any other way.

If the organization as a whole was going to move itself so far forward as to accomplish its professed One Cleveland Clinic ideal, the process absolutely demanded an authentic self-examination down to the level of our organization's DNA. Although we were facing what appeared, on the surface, to be an almost insurmountably daunting challenge, the reality, as it turned out, was that we actually had a head start because in 2007, when the initiative began gearing up, we were not starting from scratch. We were building on a body of work that had been going on since at least 1998, which was when our former CEO, Floyd Loop, MD, and his leadership team made a really big decision: that every single Cleveland Clinic patient needed to have his or her own unique Cleveland Clinic identifier. No more multiple identification numbers depending on where in the system they were being treated. No more registering and reregistering the same patients over and over again as they moved around. No more transposition or other clerical errors that were the inevitable consequence of recapturing the same data again and again. And no more Cleveland Clinic patients walking into buildings that said

Cleveland Clinic over the front door, only to be greeted as strangers.

If they were the representatives of a truly forward-thinking, state-of-the-art healthcare provider system, the members of the organization's executive leadership team decided that it was their responsibility to make the financial and labor investments necessary to position the group practice for success and growth in the coming digital age. If getting there meant starting with a single, patient-specific record for each unique patient, then they would begin by building a single technology infrastructure through which a single integrated electronic medical record system could support all the coordinated activities the group practice required.

At the time, not only was this a bold idea, it actually conflicted with much of the contemporary conventional wisdom, which said that the processes specific to delivering care in the inpatient, or hospital, setting were so completely different from the work done in the outpatient, or ambulatory, setting that if you wanted to stay out in front of the industry by implementing an electronic medical record system, you really needed two different systems because no single system could possibly take care of both.

Conventional wisdom aside, Dr. Loop and his leadership team, on which I served as the recently recruited chief information officer (CIO), decided to begin the process of envisioning the attributes of our ideal practice model by asking ourselves, "What are we really talking about here? Are we talking about taking care of a patient or a computer?"

Framed that way, the answer was immediately obvious: we're talking about taking care of patients, of *people*.

Whether a particular patient happens to be in a hospital bed, an emergency room, an ICU, a doctor's office, or a rehab unit, the way we manage and record the specifics of the care we render should be focused on that *person*, not on the setting where the care happens to take place. Therefore, the technology tools that support and coordinate our multidisciplinary work must be capable of seamlessly connecting every one of our many practice environments into a single, common cyber-care treatment space—which was most certainly *not* the industry standard at the time.

At the time, the industry adhered to a concept of selecting many different, highly specialized applications to accomplish many different, highly specific tasks called "best-in-breed," which was the direct result of ongoing incremental, often disconnected progress that had been happening on multiple fronts for years. It may have sounded good in theory, but in practice, the best-in-breed approach had a couple of underlying complications, one of which was, as an organizational solution, a stitched-together system composed of many different applications from many different vendors relied heavily on *interfaces*, which, in IT-speak, is synonymous for "places where something can break."

But this was the late 1990s. Not only was the push for increasingly integrated health systems, fully integrated IT systems, and federal "meaningful use" standards still years away, the contemporary arguments being made for the best-in-breed concept were actually quite strong. The most persuasive argument of all, at least to the leadership of a busy provider organization, was that selecting the best-in-breed technology available for a specific application would allow your clinicians to personally select exactly what they wanted.[11] And since clinicians are the soul of your business, why wouldn't you do everything in your power to accommodate their professional preferences?

In many ways, this argument was and remains so compelling that it is still energetically advocated by proponents of a kind of technology infrastructure that places a premium on qualities like nimbleness and customizability. From that perspective, it's true: no single integrated system can do absolutely everything anyone could possibly want it to do. There are fantastic niche software systems that dive very deeply into very specialized care-related activities, and these systems will always offer users who have a relatively narrow focus of interest and a high requirement for a specific functionality exactly the tools they need to do their work. There is no controversy on that point; there will always be an important place in the practice of medicine for these kinds of highly specialized applications.

But that was not what the leadership of Cleveland Clinic was trying to accomplish. We were actively building Family Health Centers, which are community-based clinical facilities that project Cleveland Clinic physician services directly into the region surrounding the main downtown campus. Connecting these new locations was a priority. Because each new community hospital that joined the system brought with it its own suite of existing technology tools, it was becoming increasingly obvious that if these organizations were going to function together like a true healthcare system, they would need to be connected through a common technical infrastructure. And that infrastructure was going to need to be big. Really big. So big that, at the time, many of the decisions about what technology applications we would adopt actually were made with the physical limitations of available computing power in mind. To build this network, we commissioned multiple IT teams to inventory existing assets, establish system operating and governance standards, select and implement common equipment so that internal variability would be kept to a minimum (thereby reducing the kinds of equipment and gear that would need to be maintained or kept in inventory), as well as a whole list of other known and soon-to-be-discovered details.

As Pam Piar, a senior IT executive[12] who has been with Cleveland Clinic since the mid-1980s, recalls, "What we learned very soon after we got this initiative up and running was that it was as much about people, and how they worked with one another, as it was about technical experience or expertise.

"We were pulling together teams from across what was, at the time, an emerging health system, and many of the people on those teams had never worked together before. A lot of them had never even met. So we had to communicate—not just amongst ourselves, as members of the IT Division, but with doctors and nurses, pharmacists and administrators, supply chain people and security personnel, everybody— because everybody had to be part of the conversation. This was a major project; probably the biggest project we had ever taken on. And to do it right, by which I mean to do it in a way that made the organization's core competency of delivering high quality healthcare easier and more efficient without risking patient safety or the functional or financial stability of the group practice, meant that it had to be done *with* the group, not *to* the group. We needed to learn how to talk to one another, how to listen to one another, and how to work with one another in ways that were, quite frankly, uncharted territory for a lot, if not most, of us."

Looking back, Pam sums up her experience as a leader during this era of intense change with one personal takeaway: "The thing I learned, and the thing I still share with the new people who join our team, is that even if our clinical colleagues don't understand anything about our world, we, as IT professionals *must understand everything about theirs*. A really important part of our job, maybe even the most important part, is understanding the needs of our clinical colleagues because it's what they do that really matters to the people who entrust their lives, and the lives of the people they love, to our care."

Mary Partin, PhD, an IT executive[13] who has also spent over 30 years of her career at Cleveland Clinic, says that, just as connecting our entire clinical operation was the network infrastructure initiative's primary parameter, Epic® was selected as the electronic medical record that would use that infrastructure after a process that balanced the present needs of the organization with future system scalability and growth.

"As the network was being designed and built out," she explains, "we were running several parallel pilot projects in several clinical locations with EMR systems from different sources. Even though, at the time, there was a lot of focus in the industry on the inpatient side of clinical practice, Dr. Harris and the team believed that it was the ambulatory side of the house that we really needed to solve first. So we decided to establish a patient's identity in the doctor's office, and then have that unique identifier stay with the patients through all the other aspects of their care instead of starting with an inpatient stay, and essentially trying to back into the ambulatory setting, which is, after all, statistically the place where the vast majority of the care a patient receives over a lifetime takes place. Unlike most other organizations, we concentrated on getting the ambulatory EMR right first."

As Adam Fogelman, a senior IT executive[14] who was a key architect of Cleveland Clinic's new IT infrastructure, recalls, the strategy quickly paid off. "When we first started this effort, it was the strategy that drove the process. Everything we did, we did with respect for the clinicians in mind. We were careful. We didn't go straight into a specialist's practice and just start ripping out applications. We created a single patient database, merged all of the patient demographic files together, and then brought all of the results from all of our hospitals into a single repository so the clinician could see the patient and the patient's results wherever they happened to be in the health system. That was the hook, really.

"On the back end, because single network servers that were powerful enough to support our entire organization inside a single box didn't yet exist, we created what we called zones, which were three closely linked mirror-like systems that each supported a geographic section of our total practice space and that, taken together, formed a single, coordinated infrastructure. By tying these zones together in a way that was almost completely invisible to the end user, we were able to approximate the experience of working inside one single network, which created something that felt very much like a single view of each individual patient. And once the single patient view became a reality for our clinicians, it wasn't long before they started saying, 'Hey, wouldn't it be great if, while I was in this patient view, I could just go ahead and place an order?' And we said, 'Sure. Absolutely. That *would* be great. That's a great idea.'"

Adam's point about respecting the people on the ground is an important one because, at the time, our senior leadership teams were asking a lot of everyone in the organization. Change can be intimidating; even change that promises great benefit can be difficult to navigate. But the clarifying moment that told us that we were legitimately on to something big came when our providers, the clinicians themselves, started actively driving the planning process for our technology road map because they experienced the tangible benefits of using an integrated network.

There were still highly specialized best-in-breed applications that we needed to implement and support. But now we talked about those specialized applications in the context of a common infrastructure that gave the entire practice environment a sense of cohesion. That was new. That was progress. And it was a testament to the willingness of everyone in the organization to come together and do the tough work that was needed to first envision what we could be, and then to actually make it happen.

This work didn't happen overnight, but it did happen. By 2007, when Dr. Cosgrove's single system vision became fully articulated as the One Cleveland Clinic initiative, not only was the technology infrastructure already substantially in place to support it but the expectations of our caregivers about what it meant to function as part of a single Cleveland Clinic care model had begun to change as well. So when "One Cleveland Clinic" became a phrase we all began to use, when the screen savers on every single workstation everywhere, regardless of location, featured the same organizational value statements; when leaders began actively encouraging their staff to look for opportunities to merge work efforts, reduce internal variability, and leverage the size of the organization as a competitive advantage instead of something that kept people apart; and when Dr. Cosgrove said, during a quarterly CEO update streamed live over our new network to all our various locations and facilities, that "everything we do, every day, whether we personally come into direct contact with patients or not, is so important that we are all, every one of us, Cleveland Clinic caregivers," it resonated.

And soon, something kind of amazing happened: One Cleveland Clinic became part of our collective consciousness—so much so that a new word spontaneously emerged that is now how we describe ourselves to ourselves: *enterprise*.

Today, Cleveland Clinic is seen by our caregivers as a single enterprise. Within the organization, the word *enterprise* has a very specific meaning. When we say *Cleveland Clinic* among ourselves, what most of us mean is the main campus plus our Family Health Centers. When we say Cleveland Clinic *health system*, we are referring to the main campus and the community hospitals. But when we say *enterprise*, we mean *all* of Cleveland Clinic.

The reason that this shared sense of enterprise identity is significant at this point in our discussion is because the connectivity of the integrated technology network and the network-delivered EMR provides every clinician the ability to instantly share information with any other clinician, anywhere, anytime; to see a patient in a Family Health Center and then to have that patient admitted to a hospital where the next doctor can simply pull up that patient's information in real time; to have operational activity data rolled up into dashboards so management can distribute resources based on demonstrable need rather than informed assumptions; and to do a thousand other things that were made possible by a standardized connectivity infrastructure, including the simple act of communicating the goals of the project using terms that turned our attention to new ways of thinking about ourselves and the work we do, which not only helped change the way Cleveland Clinic operates, it changed the way it *could* operate.

As the sense of separation created by the physical distance of our predigital reality faded into postdigital memory, Cleveland Clinic became One Cleveland Clinic. Once that sense of unity was established, there was no going back.

A New Way of Being and a New Way of Being Seen

According to the *Psychology Dictionary*, self-image is defined as the way we see ourselves.[15] It is where we find a sense of our own personality, and it is a measure against which we tend to judge our successes and shortcomings in building and maintaining relationships. Self-image can be influenced by how we choose (or are inclined) to see ourselves, how others say they see us, and how we *think* others see us, regardless of what they say.

The notion of self-*esteem* moves beyond how we see ourselves to how we *value* ourselves, and it involves judgment, subjective beliefs, and some pretty powerful emotions, such as triumph and pride, shame and despair, confidence and doubt.[16]

An even more detailed perspective on the intersection of self-image and self-esteem is called the *self-schema*, which is a grouping of both the "facts" and the beliefs we hold about who and what we are, organized into our own private personality summaries that we maintain in relation to the various circumstances of our lives. The self-schema of "I am a medical doctor," for example, contains all the expectations, beliefs, impressions, and convictions your life and experience have wrapped around your internally packaged image of "you" as a physician, which can change if, say, your hobby is playing guitar in a band on weekends, during which time you may transition to your "rock star" self-schema, however unrealistically developed it may be. When a self-schema is especially strong, it can sometimes make a person immediately self-referential whenever it is mentioned.[17] So a person who sees himself as morbidly obese is said to be self-schematic around issues of weight or eating, and this closely held belief can impact the tract and tenor of a person's life and decisions.

What's particularly interesting about the self-schema concept is that, in cognitive therapy, there are several different approaches that seek to improve the quality of a person's life by moving a self-schematic construct from being negative, and potentially harmful (I cannot control my eating no matter what I do) to one that is more positive, and therefore likely to be of benefit to the individual over time (I am a healthy eater because I want to be a healthy person).[18] The idea that by changing your mind you can consciously change some tangible aspect of your life is one of human culture's most consistent and revisited themes:

"The only thing we have to fear is fear itself."[19]

"A man without a vision is a man without a future."[20]

"Change your mind, and your life will follow."[21]

We seem to have, as self-aware creatures, an inherent appreciation for the fact that, to a great extent, *how* we see our world (and, by extension, ourselves) *is* our world.

With the decision that Cleveland Clinic would now function as one single enterprise, connected by an integrated technology infrastructure through which all common information and processes would flow and be coordinated, came the need to accomplish two perception-oriented tasks on an enormous scale:

One: we had to update and improve the self-image, self-esteem, and self-schema of every one of Cleveland Clinic's more than 40,000 employees so that they could understand, embrace, and represent this contemporary expression of the organization's original mission fully, sincerely, and proudly.

Two: we needed to introduce every existing, new, and potential patient to the twenty-first century incarnation of Cleveland Clinic's technology-connected, multidisciplinary care model in ways that would clearly articulate how these high-quality, integrated services could now be accessed and personalized in ways that would align more conveniently with their lives and needs.

We had to influence how we, and the world, saw Cleveland Clinic as an entity. How? In a word: marketing.

Charged with the dual challenge of reintroducing Cleveland Clinic to its own employees and to the patients who would potentially benefit from its improved processes and operational cohesiveness, Chief marketing officer Paul Matsen and his team found that they had access to a burgeoning online medium that the average healthcare consumer was finally beginning to really embrace and through which they could not only disseminate their value statements but even begin measuring their impact in (almost) real time. This had simply never been possible before, at least not to this degree of specificity. To get the most out of the integrated technology infrastructure that now connected the entire Cleveland Clinic enterprise internally and the new unified presence and messaging opportunities that were perfect for its external-facing web pages, the sites all needed to reflect, in every possible way, the One Cleveland Clinic philosophy.

The New Face of Healthcare Marketing: Greater Than the Sum of Its Pages

When Paul Matsen assumed responsibility for all Cleveland Clinic marketing and communications in 2006, what he found was, as he describes it, "A website. That's what I would say we had: a website. We had one. And it looked and behaved just like most other academic or university websites at the time because it was built in a very decentralized way. Every Institute, every Department, everyone, it seemed, had gone ahead and built anything they wanted, and it was all very loosely held together by some common-ish branding and navigation.

"But literally as you moved from page to page, department to department, it just wasn't unified. If you went to Primary Care, you saw one thing. If you went to the Heart Center, what you saw there was entirely different. And not only didn't we have any common tools, all of our regional hospitals had their own websites sitting on their own technical platforms. There was virtually nothing about any of them that gave visitors the impression that they were connected in any way, which was the first thing we needed to change."

Under Paul's guidance, the Marketing and Integrated Web Services team first set out to inventory and then to transition all 11,000-plus existing Cleveland Clinic web pages to a single content management system where they could be presented in a visually cohesive way, connected by the same navigational cues and logic paths, and easily accessed and updated by multiple expert content creators after only a minimal amount of common training.

As this was happening, Paul was also embarking on what became his own personal transformation. New to healthcare, his experience as the former executive vice president and chief marketing officer of Delta Airlines—which followed the years he spent at several leading New York advertising agencies earlier in his career—had firmly rooted his perspective in a style of consumer marketing that had a certain freedom of action that was just not applicable in healthcare promotion. Seizing the opportunity, Paul carefully examined his role and the role of the groups that worked for him through fresh eyes. "In healthcare marketing," he says, "there's no such thing as making any kind of an offer. There is no 'buy one get one free.' We don't offer discounts. We can't do any of those things because the people we are speaking to, our prospective patients and their families, are trusting us to help them make decisions that could potentially have significant, even momentous consequences."

Seen in this light, and considering the magnitude of the decisions a healthcare marketing team will potentially influence, it became immediately clear that it was the marketing team's primary priority—and their *responsibility*—to always represent the value the organization had to offer in as unvarnished and transparent a manner possible. That responsibility, aligned with Cleveland Clinic's "Patients First" promise, became the core of everything marketing has done ever since.

"Understanding that we live in a world full of healthcare-related information that isn't always as reliable as we might like," Paul explains, "I quickly came to realize that the Cleveland Clinic brand, our reputation, and the content we can help our experts create—that's what we have to offer.

"Through the web, we can reach people around the world with healthcare content that they can really trust. And with that being true, we thought, why would we ever do anything else? So we made it our policy that Cleveland Clinic will never buy third-party content. Everything available from Cleveland Clinic, whether it's online, in print, in a video, in a news story, in a podcast, or in a tweet, all originates with a Cleveland Clinic expert. That way, the material that starts patients on a journey that could ultimately lead them to be treated in one of our locations is always created by people who work directly with the clinicians our patients are actually coming here to see.

"And even if a patient chooses not to come to Cleveland Clinic, whether it's because of location, insurance, or for whatever reason, Cleveland Clinic experts still have the opportunity to provide information that can help that patient make a solid, informed decision."

To get that quality content to all the people who need it in ways that are impactful, meaningful, and actionable, the marketing team created what they call Cleveland Clinic's "digital ecosystem," a simplified version of which is illustrated in Figure 2.1.

The core message at the center of Cleveland Clinic's digital ecosystem is the "trusted source" information created by Cleveland Clinic experts, and then formatted specifically to fit the medium through which it will be delivered, coordinated in a way that creates an internal cohesion that ensures that, regardless of where you consume it, the underlying accuracy, tone, and personality of the material is always complemented, enhanced, and reinforced with each additional click or visit.

Also, when viewed in Figure 2.1's simplified way, an important structural feature of the digital ecosystem becomes obvious, which is that, much like the Internet itself, Cleveland Clinic's digital ecosystem is not a single "thing."

FIGURE 2.1 Cleveland Clinic's Digital Ecosystem

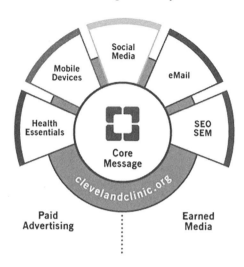

We coordinate the distribution of quality content through social media and more traditional Internet websites for an individualized healthcare marketing/health education experience.

It is an array of different applications that, together, form a connectivity network—with traditional websites, online newsletters, opt-in e-mail services, and a range of popular social media options that can all be accessed through a variety of fixed and mobile devices. It is this flexibility of choice and preference, of giving users control over what information they wish to consume and how they wish to consume it, that is the core value of the system as a whole. And like the Internet itself, the ecosystem needs constant care and feeding, the responsibility for which falls to the Health Essentials and Social Media[22] team of writers, designers, photographers, and illustrators. As the team's manager, director of content marketing Amanda Todorovich is responsible for all online content production.

"Because people use social media differently than other, more traditional forms of media," she explains, "content marketing might best be described as a 'long game,' as opposed to the 'call to action,' in-the-moment advertising that was the staple of healthcare marketing for years. When the original *Health Hub* blog was launched in 2012, the goal was to give consumers more conversational, actionable information every single day. So, every day, we published three to five articles on the blog, and our growth was tremendous. Where we started at around 200,000 visits a month, today it's not unusual for us to see four million visits a month just to the blog, which we recently renamed *Health Essentials*."

Describing the team's approach as completely data-driven, Amanda says that the core questions that are always the starting point for any strategic discussion are: Who exactly are we trying to reach? And where exactly are they during the day? Because there are so many different social media channels, both established and newly emerging, the team tracks the success of even the most nuanced details of its work, such as what are the best times of the day to do a post, how many characters in a post on a specific channel performs best, what images attract attention, and how can a post be optimized to perform to its peak of effectiveness? Through online activity tracking, unlike the slow-motion flow of information that was once the marketing professional's lot in life, today's content creators can see very clearly what material is being read and how users are engaging with it via clicks, likes, comments, and shares. By tweaking a post, changing a headline, or swapping an image, the team also learns what resonates best with their users based on real-time feedback and real consumer activity.

"Over the past few years," Amanda concludes, "social media has transitioned from being kind of supplemental in people's lives to being a focus of a lot of attention and energy. Many of these channels are well established to the point that people spend a great deal of their time engaging with the content they contain. To be successful, our team members really need to be a mix of artist and scientist. We have to be creative, but we are always data-driven. And we have to be flexible because there's never any way to know what topic is going to be hot in the moment. So we really have to listen to our audience and react to their interests with content that's appropriate, interesting, and engaging. That's the balance between art, science, and creativity."

Bridget Livengood, a manager in Cleveland Clinic's Corporate Communications and News Service, coordinates and curates news content for Cleveland Clinic's very active Twitter feed. "Even though there's this perception that, when you send something out through Twitter, Facebook, or Instagram, that it just goes out to everybody, everywhere, all at the same time," she says, "the reality is that people who use social media use it in really personal ways. Your audience is going to self-segment based on *their* personal interests. So even if it feels like you're communicating with the whole world instantly, it's important to remember that what you're really doing is giving segments of your audience an opportunity to include you in their lives. But that also means that you are giving them an equal opportunity to exclude you from their lives as well. As easily as they can let you in, they can just as easily lock you out.

"So when you understand the fundamentals of social media," Bridget concludes, "you realize that everything you do must be presented in a way that is interesting to your audience as individuals. What do they want to know? What are they thinking about? What's affecting their lives right now? If you don't think about those things, you'll lose them, maybe forever. Social media demands that you always keep your audience as the absolute center of your focus. It's not about you. It's about who you are and who you can be—to *them*."

To that end, Cleveland Clinic expresses itself in an average of 10 to 25 daily tweets generated by a creative team that is also constantly searching Twitter and other sites to discover what topics are trending, and then deciding which of those trending topics would be appropriate for one of our experts to address.

"When you really boil it down," adds Paul Matsen, "social media breaks down the barriers between people by giving us all the opportunity to selectively create relationships with new friends, with celebrities and athletes, and with the brands we prefer. In the sense that Cleveland Clinic is a healthcare brand, managing and maintaining the integrity of that brand in today's fast-paced, social media–driven world demands constant attention. You have to stay curious, and you have to stay focused.

"To do that and to do it well, you need an engaged staff of energetic people who can keep your content fresh, your presence felt, and your position relevant to the conversation that's going on right now, whatever that conversation may be. With the amount of information flowing around us and the sheer speed at which news and ideas move through the population, locally and globally one person simply cannot see everything.

"But with all the analytics tools we now have at our disposal, it's really possible to engage with people in ways that were just not viable in the pre-web world. That's why I say that, in healthcare, the whole idea of 'marketing' is changing. Today's marketing professionals have a chance to recreate the profession in a way that will make the work we do legitimately meaningful to the people who consume it.

"And like Dr. Cosgrove said, even though we aren't clinicians, we are caregivers. So if we can change the meaning of healthcare marketing to something that is focused on creating relationships with people, earning their trust, and delivering information to them that will, over time, help make their daily lives a little healthier, make their understanding of themselves and the things that can affect their well-being a little richer, and maybe even help make the process of making a difficult decision a little less stressful, then I think we will be doing justice to that caregiver ideal."

Closing the Gap

Having explored some of the ways integrated connectivity can affect an organization, its employees, and the people we serve, it is time to see how these same connectivity systems are being used to deliver healthcare services in ways that will soon change what it means to "see" your doctor. Because, even if we call the process of using technology to connect patients and clinicians in different locations "distance health," its real value is removing from the care equation the distance that separates people.

SUMMARY

1. Digital connectivity systems and tools are an important part of contemporary life, and they can have an incredible impact on the work we do and the ways we do it. Like any other tool, the potential value these systems can deliver is directly related to how they are used. Coordinated, concentrated, and objective deliberation focused on establishing a clear understanding of an organization's current state, including present technology use, as well as other mission-critical though perhaps not obviously technology-related workflows and constructs, is an important first step in creating a detailed technology road map to real change.

2. To succeed, the technology-driven transformation of any healthcare organization must be based on a comprehensive consensus position that includes the representative voices of every part of the organization's most critical resource: its people. Inclusive discussions, risk-free spaces for raising and deconstructing sensitive issues, and coordinated, ongoing, and continuous communication before, during, and after any programmatic change is essential for employee engagement and effective change management that can help avoid unnecessary mistakes, complications, or other contentious and expensive distractions and missteps.

3. The Internet's underlying relationship structure, which mirrors many of the ways human society as a whole is organized, provides an ideal vehicle through which a healthcare organization can establish and cultivate relationships with patients and their families. To be effective, everything an organization does online must be part of a carefully coordinated digital presence predicated on placing the interests of its audience at the center of everything it creates.

FIGURE 2.2 The Integrated Technology Services Value Equation

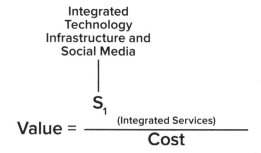

The first major functional category of Integrated Technology Services is the infrastructure required to connect people inside an organization, a medical practice, and in an online, constantly-developing social media community ecosystem.

Bottom Line

As an extension of the reach of our ideas and imagination, information technology tools open up new vistas of possibility and potential. This expanded horizon itself can fundamentally change what we know, what we do, and who we ultimately aspire to be.

High-Tech, High-Touch

Time Is Brain

Dr. Irene Katzan was about to step into exam room S8-211 to see the next patient on her morning's schedule, a 72-year-old woman who had experienced a transient ischemic attack (TIA) nine days before, when the pager in the right hip pocket of her white clinician's smock vibrated. She read the message, MOBILE STROKE UNIT EN ROUTE 10 MINUTES, and clipped the device onto her coat.

As a staff physician in Cleveland Clinic's Neurological Institute, Dr. Katzan specializes in cerebrovascular disease and secondary stroke prevention (the word *prevention* occupies a prominent position in her clinical philosophy). Even though the distinction between a stroke (the presence of focal neurological deficits that last for more than 24 hours) and a TIA (deficit symptoms lasting less than 24 hours)[1] may, in recent years, have begun losing some of its importance given how effective the same preventative approaches have become for treating either condition, to Dr. Katzan, preventing a stroke is clearly the preferred approach for minimizing the damage it can inflict. And preventing damage was also the reason she kept a special pager in her right hip pocket.

Nicknamed the "clot" pager, it only went off for one reason: someone was in the process of having a stroke. In about 10 minutes, she would be treating that patient, wherever the patient happened to be in a surrounding area of about 100 square miles.

Since her next patient was already roomed, Dr. Katzan asked her physician's assistant (PA) to go ahead and start taking vitals while she excused herself and walked down a hall in Cleveland Clinic's second oldest building toward a room that contained some of the organization's newest equipment. As she did, her clot pager vibrated a second time, and the display read, ON SCENE DROP ORDERS, followed by an electronic medical record number (eMRN).

Leaving the lights dim, Dr. Katzan sat down at a computer workstation that had two very large high-definition flat-screen monitors positioned side by side that could either display information independently or be quickly configured to work as one big screen. Logging in to the MyPractice electronic health record system, she entered the eMRN she had been sent and found that the 66-year-old male patient she was about to treat was already established, meaning he had received care from a Cleveland Clinic provider in the past. (One convenient feature of the Mobile Stroke Treatment Unit program, which had been functional for almost one year, was that even if the patient had been new to Cleveland Clinic, there was a process in place through which that new patient would have been registered, on the fly, in real time.)

Though, on the outside, the Mobile Stroke Treatment Unit may look like an ordinary ambulance, on the inside it is actually a million-dollar, specially designed rolling stroke-specific emergency department equipped with a portable computerized tomography (CT) machine and staffed by a CT tech, a paramedic, an emergency medical technician (EMT), and a critical care nurse. To date, it had been treating acute stroke cases all across Cleveland so successfully that several adjacent cities had recently asked to be added to the unit's area of operation.

The original idea for the Mobile Stroke Treatment Unit came from a pilot program in Michigan, as well as a 2012 German study of 100 patients who showed a significant decrease in both the time to diagnosis and the time to administration of clot dissolving drugs[2] when the initial intervention was delivered on-site by a specialized team using the right equipment. In the case of ischemic stroke, which is a stroke caused when an obstruction blocks an artery that supplies blood to the brain,[3] a patient can lose as many as two million brain cells a minute. So the more quickly treatment begins, the less damage may be done, which can be the differentiator between a mild, temporary problem and a major, potentially permanent disability resulting in the pain, suffering, and loss associated with a diminished quality of life as well as a significant cost for lifetime care.

Quickly reviewing the patient's information in MyPractice, Dr. Katzan wrote and submitted an order for a CT scan that would be done immediately, right there in the ambulance. Both the CT image and its interpreted result would be very important to the treatment decisions she was about to make. This was a major difference between the workflow associated with the Mobile Stroke Treatment Unit and another more well-established technology-connected clinical program called Telestroke, through which Cleveland Clinic stroke specialists supported emergency departments all across northern Ohio and western Pennsylvania. Emergency departments (EDs) that contracted with Cleveland Clinic for Telestroke coverage had a direct audiovisual link to on-call stroke specialists who could add their specialty expertise to the general ED physician's treatment activities. But in Telestroke, the contracted specialist was considered a consultant and the ED clinician the treating physician. In the Mobile Stroke Treatment Unit, Dr. Katzan was the treating physician of record.

After a few minutes an alert popped up on the left flat-screen, notifying her that the CT images were available to be viewed in MyPractice, which is what Cleveland Clinic calls its highly customized version of the EHR system available from Epic.

Because Epic provides a wide range of different technology modules that perform a variety of activities (patient registration, scheduling, documentation, etc.), clients have the option of aligning and arranging the modules they need to accomplish the practice-specific tasks they conduct in exactly the way they choose. Cleveland Clinic first began using Epic in 2001, so the number of clinician-directed, best-practice-related modifications, customized order-set build-outs, and specialty-specific enhancements that have been made to the system over time have resulted in a version of the Epic EHR product that is uniquely our own. As a way of distinguishing our version of the system from those used by other providers, we brand our practice-optimized version MyPractice on every page through which it can be accessed, including those that appear on the office workstations of the several hundred regional physicians in private practice who contract with us to lease the MyPractice Community version of the system.

By the time her iPhone started ringing, Dr. Katzan's quick review of the CT images told her pretty much everything she needed to know. As she answered the phone, her clot pager went off for the third time, displaying, READY FOR DOC. Before she turned on the flat-screen to her right, she reviewed the report with the neuroradiologist who had just uploaded it, which confirmed Dr. Katzan's initial impression that the scans did not show any intracranial bleeding—which was good. Bleeding was what you would expect to see in the case of a ruptured artery or aneurysm (hemorrhagic stroke), which would have made this an entirely different and potentially even more acutely serious situation. Also, since neither she nor the neuroradiologist could see any evidence of an obvious blockage, not unusual given that a tiny blockage inside an artery is often not visible on the first CT taken after a neurovascular event, she understood that she was probably treating an ischemic stroke that had occurred very recently.

Switching off her phone and turning on the right-side flat-screen, Dr. Katzan watched as the monitor displayed what was going on inside the Mobile Stroke Unit—which was parked in the patient's driveway.

It was an early spring morning. The weather was mild and the sun was out. The patient had been mowing his lawn for the first time that year, and his wife found him confused and acting strangely, sitting on the ground with his back against the driver's side door of his car, the mower whining unattended on the grass. That's when she called 911. The 911 dispatcher alerted the Mobile Stroke Treatment Unit.

"Hello," Dr. Katzan said, raising a hand to wave as she said the patient's name. "I'm Dr. Irene Katzan, a stroke neurologist from Cleveland Clinic. And we're seeing you here today because there's some concern that you may have had a stroke. We need to ask you some questions. Would that be all right? Can you answer some questions? Is that your wife? Yes? Hello. I'm Dr. Katzan. Now, can you tell me the last time you felt well? Do you do know how long it has been since you felt well?"

From there, the process took only a few minutes. Carefully watching her patient's facial and other reactions, Dr. Katzan quickly conducted a standardized examination utilizing the National Institutes of Health Stroke Scale (NIHSS), a set of 15 focus areas that help physicians score the effect of an acute cerebral infarction (obstruction) on a patient's level of consciousness, responsiveness, alertness, eye movement, motor abilities, facial and limb weakness, ability to use language, and ability to pay attention to what was happening in the moment.

Quickly excluding the possibility that her patient was suffering from delirium or was intoxicated or otherwise chemically impaired, and after verifying that he was not presently taking any prescription blood thinners, did not have a history of bleeding, had not been diagnosed as having had another stroke within the past three months, and that his present blood pressure was not significantly elevated, she concluded that he was at risk for stroke-related damage and did not have any contraindicators that would exclude the use of intravenous tissue plasminogen activator (tPA), which is the only FDA-approved treatment for ischemic stroke in the United States.[4]

"I would say," she said, "that based on the examination we just completed and from the findings of your CT scan, it looks like you're in the middle of having the kind of stroke that is caused by a blocked blood vessel in your brain. Today, we have a treatment available called intravenous tPA, which is a clot-busting medication that we can give you, first as an injection, and then in an IV. The purpose of this medication is to break up the blood clot that we think is preventing your blood from flowing freely, which is what will damage the cells in your brain.

"Now there is a risk with this intervention, which is why we looked very carefully at your CT and why we asked you all those questions. But we think that you're a good candidate for this medication, and studies have shown that people who get it do better than those who do not. We can probably increase the odds that you will be left with little or no permanent disability by about 30 percent if you receive this medication. The thing we worry about most with it is bleeding within the brain, which can sometimes be very serious, even fatal. But even taking that risk into account, generally people do better if they receive this medication, and it is our standard of care.

"Do you understand what I just explained to you? OK. That's good. So, do you want to receive this medication?"

When the patient agreed that he would go ahead with the IV-tPA, the Mobile Stroke Team, who had already gotten his weight as part of their original examination, injected the first bolus dose and set up the IV to get the infusion that would last for about an hour started. Once the IV bag was hanging in place, they set off for the closest ED, having cut at least 30 minutes from the time it would have taken to start the intervention. And since, as they say in stroke neurology, "time is brain," the likelihood of a positive outcome for the patient and his family hopefully would be improved accordingly.

Switching off the camera screen, Dr. Katzan took a few minutes to complete her note in the MyPractice EHR and, because IV-tPA was involved, she made a quick phone call to apprise the ED physicians who would be receiving the patient within the next few minutes of the treatment she had already delivered. Then she closed the EHR encounter, cleared her clot pager, turned off the workstation, and returned to what she had been doing—which was caring for her next patient, who was waiting in exam room S8-211.

A Technology Solution to a Technology Problem?

It's one of the oldest dilemmas in medicine: how do physicians balance the need to create personal relationships with their patients during which they have sufficient time to gather all the critical information they need against the necessity of treating as many patients as possible in a way that is cost-effective enough to keep healthcare affordable for all? How do doctors make and maintain those all-important human connections, nurture those interpersonal relationships, and get to know and understand their patients as people, even as the overwhelming economic and practice management pressures of a high-volume marketplace demand that they conduct "encounters" that look more like automated stops on an assembly line than personalized expert consultations?

In modern medical practice, the reality is that today's clinicians are constantly being driven to move their patients along as quickly as they can. So it should come as no surprise that the unrelenting pressure, pace, and volume of their work can often lead to cynicism, burnout, and frustration. Equally, patients can quickly come to feel that they are not so much the recipients of the caring attention of concerned professionals as they are functional units of time for which bills can be generated and fees collected. The entire activity of caring for the sick, which is a pure expression of simple human compassion, can become a complicated Gordian knot of competing priorities and untethered emotions.

How can a finite number of doctors take care of what must feel like an infinite number of patients in a way that works for everyone? How do we deliver high-quality healthcare while maintaining a quality of life for the individuals who provide that care that is commensurate with the responsibility they are willing to assume, while still earning the confidence and trust of those they treat—without which there can be no healthcare system at all? How can everyone have everything they need all the time without any of us ever having to worry about what it costs or if there is actually enough of it to go around?

It is becoming increasingly clear that one of the key factors that began driving a wedge between doctors and their patients, the availability of increasingly advanced medical technology, may actually be part of the solution to the problem that technology itself helped create.

Consider the arc of medical practice in the United States, which began with doctors paying house calls to the sick. Three major factors helped shift the standard model of highly personalized—if generalized—care delivered directly in the patient's home by a visiting physician who had everything he needed in his "little black bag" to a model that increasingly asked sick people to visit their more specialized doctors in their offices or in the hospital.[5]

It was the combination of industrialization,[6] with the increased concentration of people into larger and larger cities wherein even those with few marketable skills were promised the opportunity of factory-based employment, and the Civil War, which presented the American medical community with a more-than-ample opportunity to learn how to treat a variety of serious, contractible diseases, physical trauma, and overwhelming emotional distress,[7] that began the move toward hospital-based care. At more or less the same time, physicians were also learning to rely on a whole new suite of emerging medical technologies, such as laboratory tests and the particularly wondrous x-ray machine,[8] which pushed their clinical expectations toward organizations in which diagnostic and other technologies could be concentrated[9] (as opposed to the far less efficient arrangement of trying to lug such equipment around, as was briefly the style during an experimental period of American healthcare know as Railway Medicine, when mobile hospital cars visited the cities and towns located along the routes of the nation's ever-expanding network of train tracks).[10]

Access to technology was a significant contributing factor in creating what ultimately became our presently accepted approach to healthcare delivery in which clinicians are concentrated around fixed hospital locations that contain the equipment they need and use. But now, through a growing current of secure, Internet-based services, we are beginning to see yet another shift in the structure of care delivery that is making an updated version of the more traditional house-call-based, personalized medical model our great-grandparents may have known an increasingly viable option for both patients and providers.

At Cleveland Clinic, these innovative services are being expressed through a range of programs such as Telestroke, the Mobile Stroke Unit, our OR of the Future, and eHospital programs. Regardless of their present level of technical sophistication, all of these services can trace their lineage directly back to a single starting point that we once called E-Cleveland Clinic.

The "E-Volution" of Medical Practice (It Sounded a Lot Cooler in 1999)

The initial idea was fairly simple: there are diagnoses for which, even if a patient traveled to see a Cleveland Clinic specialist for a second medical opinion, that specialist would still use pathology slides, x-ray films, laboratory tests, and other technology-based diagnostic information as the foundation of his or her opinion. So in these specific situations, why not just send the x-ray or the slide to Cleveland? Why make the patient come, too, especially since he or she would not be feeling well?

That's how E-Cleveland Clinic was originally conceived. Well, that was the genesis of the remote second opinion service that has since come to be known as MyConsult. The E-Cleveland Clinic name had more to do with what was going on in the consumer marketplace at the time than it did with any medical requirements. In the late 1990s, there were an awful lot of *Es* floating around, including the E-CRMS (electronic customer relationship management systems) that promised to enhance your E-retail, E-banking, E-health, and other E-business opportunities in ways that were guaranteed to help you make an E-normous (I made that last one up) splash in the brave new world of E-commerce. All you had to do was send them an E-mail. So why not E-Cleveland Clinic? But what exactly was E-Cleveland Clinic?

Originally, it was our online, remote second medical opinion service through which patients could visit a website and search to see if the diagnosis they were facing was included in what started out as a list of about 300 life-threatening or life-altering diagnoses for which a Cleveland Clinic specialist could render an online second opinion in a reasonable period of time. Naturally, the original diagnosis list—which has since grown to over 1,200 diagnoses—was heavy on cancer, heart disease, and other conditions that are identified mostly through the interpretation of diagnostic tests. Though it was not the first service of its kind in the country, its distinguishing feature was that it was conducted at the direction of and in direct cooperation with the patient.

The service was first called "high-tech and high-touch" by its medical director, Jonathan Schaffer, MD, an orthopedic surgeon who was recruited back to his hometown of Cleveland because of his experience in applying Internet-based technologies to change the face of healthcare. "While it is our goal to use technology to bring patients and clinicians together," read some of our earliest program description materials, "we must never lose sight of the fact that the basis of the entire healthcare experience is the trust a patient places in their doctor."

Since it is impossible to replicate the feeling of speaking to another human being, of actually hearing the person's voice as he or she answers your questions, and of exchanging information in a personal way that gives you the time you need to understand fully the details of whatever you are discussing, the team charged with developing the E-Cleveland

Clinic system made a point of engineering direct telephone contact between the patient and a nurse, anytime the patient wanted it, as a hardwired component of the service's primary workflow.

"Right from the start," says Sue Omori, E-Cleveland Clinic's first marketing manager, who was an important part of the development team, "we decided that what we did *not* want to build was a service that asked a patient to just fill out some forms online. Instead, we consciously set out to create an experience that would make the patient feel connected to real people, who were doing real work on his or her behalf. So while we wanted to make the more mechanical tasks associated with transferring the information our doctors needed as simple as possible, we also knew that what would set E-Cleveland Clinic apart was that human connection. That was always the driving motivation for everything we did."

Following many discussions with clinicians in various specialties, the team developed a series of detailed workflows outlining everything that would need to happen, from the first moment a patient initiated the online request process through the time a doctor was finally presented with the case. Understanding how valuable a clinician's time can be, particularly a highly specialized physician treating complex and difficult conditions, the team knew that if the E-Cleveland Clinic remote second opinion process was ever going to be adopted as a standard part of Cleveland Clinic's busy specialty practice, the material a doctor received would need to be as complete, accurate, and organized as possible.

These efforts eventually resulted in what came to be known as the "pizza box," a standardized, color-coded container that presented everything the clinicians who first agreed to participate in the program said they needed in exactly the way they needed to see it. No incomplete case would ever arrive on a physician's desk, and no physician would ever waste time digging through a jumbled stack of photocopied notes, looking for missing images or results.

There was also the matter of physician licensing and how it applied in situations where a patient who resided in one state was requesting an interaction with a physician who was located in another state or medical licensing jurisdiction. In almost every case, state law mandated that if a patient chose to consult with an out-of-state physician who had never physically seen that patient, the physician needed to be licensed to practice medicine in the patient's state of residence. That was the law in most states. There were others that would not allow (and some that still do not allow) interstate online medical consultations at all. There was also the matter of compensation since, at the time, there were virtually no available private (or public) health insurance products that would recognize an Internet consultation as a legitimate, or "billable," medical interaction. And finally, there was the future.

First, this work was happening at the same time the IT Division was kicking off our systemwide single network infrastructure initiative that already had, as one of its most important parts, several EHR pilot programs up and running. Any documentation generated by the E-Cleveland Clinic remote second opinion service would need to be included in whatever electronic health record system we would finally select, allowing us to redefine what it meant to become a Cleveland Clinic patient by creating a new registered *virtual* patient category—a novel concept in 2001.

Second, if the service really did catch on, which was our firm belief, it would need to be built from the start in a way that would be scalable, so it could handle a high volume of cases without causing an increase in the time our patients would be expected to wait for an opinion to be rendered.

Third, we needed a website, but not just any website. We wanted the E-Cleveland Clinic service to be as personal as possible. We wanted our patients to be able to keep track of how their second opinions were progressing (not unlike the popular "track package" feature that is now a standard part of nearly every purchase customers make online).

By 2000, we had completed our preparatory and planning work, but to get to where we wanted to go, we realized that we were going to need some pretty serious help. We found it in Dallas, Texas, at the Health Information Management Systems Society annual conference, where we happened to run into the very dynamic Ross Perot on the convention floor.

What We Really Need Is a Partner

Perhaps best known for his two presidential runs, the first as an independent candidate in 1992 and the second as the Reform Party candidate in 1996,[11] American businessman and entrepreneur Ross Perot founded Perot Systems in 1988.[12] Headquartered in Plano, Texas, from its first day in business to when it was acquired by Dell Inc. for $3.9 billion in 2009,[13] Perot Systems was a leading provider of information technology services to several industries, including banking, manufacturing, insurance, and healthcare.[14]

Founded in 1961 at the Georgia Institute of Technology, the Health Information Management Systems Society (HIMSS) has more than 52,000 members, more than two-thirds of whom work in healthcare, government, and not-for-profit organizations around the world.[15] The annual national convention that HIMSS holds in the United States regularly attracts more than 20,000 attendees and features an enormous convention floor that has become one of the world's premier IT vendor spaces.

Given the popularity of HIMSS events, it should come as no surprise that representatives from Cleveland Clinic and Perot Systems were both in attendance that year in Dallas.

What was propitious, recalls Joe Turk, senior director for new business development in Cleveland Clinic's IT Division, who, at the time, was a Perot Systems regional relationship manager, was how naturally the two groups seemed to connect. "As I remember it," he says, "it all started with Dr. Harris and his group talking to our Perot team on the convention floor about this idea they had been working on for a second opinion service that patients could use online. Ross Perot, who happened to be attending the conference that year, heard about what Cleveland Clinic was doing, and he and Dr. Harris got together and had a conversation that resulted in Perot Systems working up a conceptual framework that Cleveland Clinic eventually adopted.

"For its time, it was a very novel approach; it was very much a working partnership. So much so that Perot Systems actually became one of the first companies to contract with E-Cleveland Clinic to provide the online second opinion service as part of their employees' health benefits package. I was the relationship manager for the project, which was so important to us that I ended up actually moving to Cleveland from Texas. I started working for Cleveland Clinic in 2004, which was when we finally moved the whole system onto Cleveland Clinic's integrated infrastructure platform."

The solution that Joe and the Perot Systems team originally built in partnership with the E-Cleveland Clinic development group was customized to conduct all the online transactions necessary to complete a remote second opinion, from presenting the list of available diagnoses to displaying the biographies of the Cleveland Clinic physician specialists who would be doing the work; from keeping track internally of the various states in which the E-Cleveland Clinic team had secured and maintained medical licenses for their physicians to delivering the text of the finalized opinion those physicians completed; from password protecting the confidentiality of our patients to the security and functionality required to enter credit card information and pay for a service, making the site unique for its time.

That last feature, the ability to use a credit card for patients who were not employed by a company that offered the service as part of their healthcare benefits, would prove to be particularly important to the growth and success of the program. While our original business development strategy focused on cultivating corporate clients, it was average consumers who embraced the service as their own.

Following several months during which the new business development team visited a number of large corporations around the country, E-Cleveland Clinic was contractually included in the health benefits packages of several of our nation's most prominent commercial enterprises. By the start of 2001, the service was up and running, actively delivering online second opinions to patients in a progressively expanding region, beginning with Ohio and neighboring states. We also began receiving international requests through Cleveland Clinic's Global Patient Services team. With each new patient and each new experience, we were learning and improving the process and the product.

As our volume grew, the time approached when we knew that we would need to introduce E-Cleveland Clinic to the general consumer market. As a premier tertiary care center, Cleveland Clinic engages with many physicians from all across the country who entrust their patients to us for specialty interventions. We therefore needed to be scrupulous about not creating any promotional or marketing materials that could be construed as an attempt to impinge upon the practices or reputation of our physician colleagues.

We decided we would not advertise our service in any local newspapers or region-specific media because such a placement potentially could be seen as an attempt to compete directly with the local physician community. That was precisely *not* what the E-Cleveland Clinic service was meant to do. From the start, in addition to empowering patients, it was our goal to make E-Cleveland Clinic an easy-to-access way of creating and enhancing collaborative physician relationships. Through a convenient and efficient structure, we wanted to streamline the consultative process in a way that would allow physicians everywhere to include Cleveland Clinic specialty expertise, and when a patient's unique circumstances required it, our specialty care, in the comprehensive service set they could provide to their own local patient populations.

Just as our original development of the E-Cleveland Clinic service's technical infrastructure had led to a close, collaborative partnership with Perot Systems, we hoped that by making the consultative expertise of our specialty clinicians available to patients and their physicians anytime through a clear and reliable process, we could develop effective clinical partnerships with physicians around the world that would enhance and focus the individual strengths we each had to offer.

But it was not going to be easy to explain what we could do. At a time (2000 to 2002) when only about 6 percent of Americans had access to high-speed broadband Internet at home,[16] and of the 45 percent of Americans who actually used the Internet, only 8.1 percent conducted any kind of online banking activity,[17] communicating the idea that you could now use that same Internet to accomplish a real, clinically valid healthcare encounter in simple, convincing language that would impact the potential preferences of an already stressed, recently diagnosed patient audience was, to put it mildly, a challenge.

In 2003, following several intense rounds of focus groups, surveys, discussions, and reviews, the first national advertisement for the E-Cleveland Clinic second medical opinion service appeared in *U.S.A. Today*, a publication that we

FIGURE 3.1 E-Cleveland Clinic's First National Consumer
Advertisement

It announced an online service through which patients could "Travel to
The Cleveland Clinic for a second opinion without leaving home."

selected because it was not associated with any one particular
region of the country. As Figure 3.1 shows, the ad was quite
serious in tone, relatively heavy in explanatory text, and, by
today's standards, long. But it worked. Almost immediately,
interest in the service increased, leading to calls from patients
and organizations all across the country that eventually led to
the presidential visit discussed in this book's opening pages.

In 2004, with the E-Cleveland Clinic program expanding both the volume of patients we served and the kinds of

services we could provide, a brief programmatic description was included in the messages callers heard as they waited for their calls to Cleveland Clinic's main telephone number to be transferred to the correct department or party. One day, a reporter for a highly regarded national newspaper called to conduct a telephone interview with one of our cardiologists. While she waited for the doctor to come on the line, she heard the E-Cleveland Clinic "on-hold" message. She was so intrigued that she went on to write what would become a front-page article about how E-Cleveland Clinic, and several other Internet-based medical services offered by healthcare organizations around the country, were beginning to gain traction in the public's consciousness.

It was that article that was, among other things, referenced by the White House advance person who contacted us in the first week of January 2005 regarding the intention of the president to visit Cleveland Clinic to discuss how technology could improve medical practice.

Another result of this increase in consumer interest was the realization within our internal operations team and among many of our organization's thought leaders that the E-Cleveland Clinic idea was much bigger than we had originally imagined.

The first obvious indication that we needed to revise our thinking, as well as the definition of the term, came when we added personalized counseling by a board-certified nutritionist to the E-Cleveland Clinic list of services. Adding a new service required a complete web redesign because, by definition, a nutrition consultation was not a second opinion. We had also been approached with the idea of offering situation-specific preadoptive consultations for parents who were planning to welcome a child into their lives. These consults would allow parents the opportunity to outline everything they knew about the child they were about to adopt so that a Cleveland Clinic pediatrician could help them plan what they would need to do to help their children meet their developmental milestones and receive any specialized attention they might require in order to thrive in their new home. That service would also require a website redesign, so we made a rather significant transition.

What we had been branding as E-Cleveland Clinic, the secure, online second medical opinions we offered to corporate clients and consumers, now became MyConsult. E-Cleveland Clinic was reformatted to eCleveland Clinic, and used to describe any medical service we delivered through an information technology–enabled process or platform.

An online portal through which physicians who referred a patient to Cleveland Clinic for specialty care could log in and see everything that was documented in our EHR related to that patient's progress all the way through the treatment process, in real time, free of cost, and with their patients' consent was called eCleveland Clinic DrConnect.[18]

An online portal that connected our patients to portions of their own electronic health records, including the results of laboratory and other tests, their prescribed medications, their medication allergies, their demographic information, and upcoming and past appointments was called eCleveland Clinic MyChart.[19]

An integrated electronic health record system, refined and refocused by ongoing clinician input to be as comprehensive and user-friendly as possible, available in every facility, office, and location to connect the entire clinical enterprise in a single digital practice environment, was called eCleveland Clinic MyPractice.[20]

And so on (as depicted in Figure 3.2).

It was a game changer. It made us realize that we were not limited to using the Internet to accomplish just one new idea. We were changing the way we perceived the role of information

FIGURE 3.2 eCleveland Clinic eHealth Services

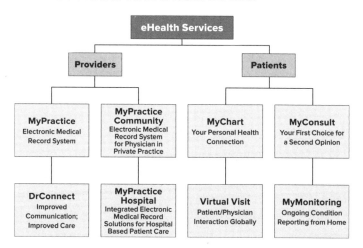

These services were customized for providers and patients, integrated for enterprise adoption and availability, and branded to distinguish the technical nature of our design and help catalyze a transformation in the way providers and patients think about service delivery and potential.

technology as part of our practice, thereby increasing the potential depth and reach of almost everything we did. And while the brand eCleveland Clinic could not last, its demise in 2010 was itself a milestone. While we had all originally agreed that we needed a descriptor that would clearly differentiate these services in the minds of our patients and provider colleagues, a term that would be easy to remember and that would immediately call out the value and power of the work that was helping us reach out to people around the world, what we came to realize was that these services were not separate from our practice at all. These services *were* our practice.

Karen Jensen, BSN, RN, who has been with Cleveland Clinic for more than 30 years and who has served as the nurse manager of MyConsult Clinical Operations since 2008, makes this clear when she talks about the work she and her team are asked to do. "Everyone thinks it's just about the technology, but it's really not," she says, indicating a row of six workstations located on the other side of her office window in the MyConsult Clinical Operations center, at which six different telephone calls are in progress. "Since I've been here, our volume has more than doubled, with requests coming in from literally all over the world. We've done remote second opinions for patients in over 100 countries. But it wasn't the technology that made that happen, it was our team, and the doctors who reach out to patients who need their experience and skill. Because that's what this is all about. It's about talking to our patients and providing that personalized touch that sets this service apart.

"We talk to our patients every step of the way, and in the process, we get to know them as people. Like Monte Riley and his wife, Sandi. They were just here. They just knocked on our door, and even though we had never met in person, it was like we were long-lost friends. It was like a reunion; it was so emotional. Did I tell you his story?"

Monte Riley, age 51, and his wife, Sandi, are residents of Oklahoma who decided to explore their healthcare options after Monte's heart murmur was no longer asymptomatic. Monte's doctor originally detected his heart murmur during an annual physical, which came as quite a surprise. "I didn't have any symptoms at all that I was aware of," Monte says. "But I was having a routine checkup when my doctor said, 'You need to see a cardiologist right away,' which I did, only to be told that I needed a new mitral valve and a new aortic valve immediately."

On the advice of a nurse practitioner who was his wife's close friend, Monte saw another local cardiologist who helped him postpone surgery for about four years through a regimen of heart medications, blood thinners, and careful monitoring that included an echocardiogram every six months. But finally, as they knew would eventually happen, Monte began experiencing symptoms, and his doctor said that it was time to act.

Because he needed a surgeon who not only had experience with heart valve repair but also had the very specialized skills needed to address Monte's pectus excavatum (a congenital abnormal development of the rib cage in which the breast-bone grows inward, causing compression of the heart and lungs),[21] he and his wife went online, looking for information. When they found Cleveland Clinic's MyConsult service, they began collecting his medical information in preparation for Monte's second opinion consultation.

"I must have called the nurses at the MyConsult office a billion times with questions," Sandi, says. "It was a really stressful time in our lives. I'm sure they have thousands of patients each year from all over the world, yet they always made me feel as if we were their only patients. They were so prompt and helpful. I felt like we had our own personal care team throughout the process."

After Monte and Sandi sent in the necessary information, the MyConsult nursing team delivered it to Stephanie Mick, MD, a cardiovascular surgeon in the Department of Thoracic and Cardiovascular Surgery. Two weeks later, Monte and Sandi received Dr. Mick's report.

"I thought it was great," he says. "I felt like her opinion was very comprehensive. When we sent in our follow-up questions, she responded right away and answered as if we were sitting right there in her office. She knew exactly what needed to be done and who needed to be involved for my surgery, should I decide to go to Cleveland. We sought opinions from a few other healthcare systems, but based on our experience with MyConsult, we felt confident that Cleveland Clinic was where we needed to be."

"I was extremely overwhelmed with emotion and started crying when I saw the Cleveland Clinic from the airplane's window," recalls Sandi. "I said, 'Monte, I think these people are going to be able to fix you. I really believe you're going to be OK!'"

Dr. Mick and Daniel Raymond, MD, also of the Department of Thoracic and Cardiovascular Surgery, performed an aortic and mitral valve replacement, a tricuspid valve repair, and a rebuild of Monte's chest wall to repair his pectus excavatum.

Monte and Sandi spent about two weeks at Cleveland Clinic while Monte recovered from his surgery, and finally, when he could, they decided that there was something special they wanted to do.

"We stopped in to meet the MyConsult nursing team and thank them for all they had done for us," Sandi says. "Although we had only spoken over the phone, we felt like we already knew them. Now that we're back in Oklahoma, we keep in touch and we send them regular updates on Monte's progress."

At last report, Monte was back at work, and looking forward to getting out on the golf course soon.

"When we first met him," Karen says, "Monte could barely talk because he was so touched to meet the people who had helped him. It was so heartwarming; it's just so gratifying. It's probably the best part of our job. But it's not unique. We call it a remote second opinion, but there's nothing remote about it. It's very personal, like all healthcare is personal. And even though we don't always get to meet our patients in person, we always get to know them. And we care about them very much. It's a unique dynamic, and I think there is just so much more that we will be able to do with it in the future."

Karen's closing observation brings us to a very interesting point of clarity. A program called Distance Health is actually about eliminating the distance between people. For her, the computer and the telephone are sufficient to accomplish a real connection between her patients and her team. But for Peter Rasmussen, MD, an interventional endovascular neurosurgeon, the Distance Health program he now directs has barely gotten started.

Doing Better Starts with Doing

Dr. Rasmussen's interest in telemedicine goes back at least 15 years, when it became obvious to him that there was room to improve the way stroke patients were receiving care in emergency situations. It was this desire to "do better," as he describes it, that led him to become one of the leading voices behind the Cleveland Clinic's Cerebrovascular Vascular Center's efforts to develop what would eventually become the Cleveland Clinic Telestroke Network—the progenitor of the Mobile Stroke Treatment Unit we encountered at the beginning of this chapter.

"As a development process," says Dr. Rasmussen, "Telestroke happened in parallel to the development of stroke neurology as a real area of clinical specialty in neurological practice. Because years ago and continuing even today, the vast majority of stroke patients in this country are managed by general neurologists."

As a field, neurology is very broad, with many areas of specialty, such as headache, dementia, movement disorders, and sleep and cognitive conditions. As stroke neurology became a codified specialty and proven treatments for stroke were developed and improved, it quickly became clear that there just weren't enough stroke specialists available to meet patient needs—especially since, in the case of acute stroke, time is such a critical factor in the effectiveness of stroke interventions.

Cleveland Clinic's Telestroke model features what Dr. Rasmussen calls the "mother ship" or the "hub" of care, which is where the expert clinicians reside. At first, the hub was on Cleveland Clinic's main campus, but later, as mobile technologies improved and the all-important availability of 4G networks increased, the idea of the hub itself became more fluid, moving to the specialist's office, then the home, and eventually, like so much else, to the smartphone.

Radiating out from the central clinician hub are portable telemedicine kiosks, which serve as instantaneous, real-time connection points between an emergency department location, the ED physician, the patient, and the stroke neurologist. For those hospitals that contract with Cleveland Clinic for Telestroke support, contact with the stroke specialist happens in about three to five minutes. This is critical because, while the signs and symptoms of stroke can sometimes be quite obvious, they can also be more subtle, making a rapid diagnosis trickier and potentially increasing the time to treatment.

Given the ticking clock aspect of an acute stroke encounter, it may come as something of a surprise that Dr. Rasmussen credits the MyConsult remote second opinion service as one of the models he had in mind as he worked on both the Telestroke service and the Mobile Stroke Treatment Unit.

"I've been doing MyConsult second opinions for years," he says, "and I think of MyConsult as a slower-paced version of doing a Telestroke interaction. You know, there are multiple ways you can do distance health. The potential of virtual medicine is really only limited by your imagination and your desire to actually *do* something. You can do a very rapid connection, like what we do for acute ischemic stroke—because, as a defined singular diagnosis, it's easy for us to make sure we have the right provider available to handle it. Or you can do a connection like MyConsult, which excels because it makes such a wide funnel of actionable diagnoses available to our patients. But because that range is so wide, it takes some time to connect the right patient to the right provider, but it's that connection, of the right patient and the right doctor, that is also the heart of a Telestroke interaction, and it's what the Mobile Stroke Treatment Unit is all about, too. We just had to wait to initiate our programs because we needed the technology to mature."

What they needed, Dr. Rasmussen explains, was for everything on their specialized Telestroke kiosk carts, especially the audio and video connection equipment—that was itself a real innovation—to be condensed into a small, portable form. Then they needed a ubiquitous, 4G-level wireless network to get their live video connections working. Finally, for the Mobile Stroke Treatment Unit, they needed a portable CT scanner that was small enough to fit inside a vehicle but robust enough to be bounced around on the road. The same was true for the portable point-of-care laboratory testing equipment and all the other rapid deployment medical devices that make the Mobile Stroke Treatment Unit such a capable, self-contained, continually connected interventional asset.

"Just like the original process of mapping out all their critical steps and aligning the technology they needed to either buy or build that the MyConsult team went through as they were designing their service," Dr. Rasmussen says, "we did the same kind of work when we created our Telestroke and Mobile Stroke Treatment Unit programs. And also, just like MyConsult had its fair share of skeptics early on, we had voices saying that what we were proposing was too expensive or, in the case of the Mobile Stroke Treatment Unit, that an emergency squad could get a patient to a hospital faster, and that was really what we should be worried about measuring.

"But when you think about it, is it really that expensive? How about the alternatives? Is it really too expensive when you think about the alternative of patients not getting the care they need quickly enough, patients who could potentially be paralyzed and need constant care for the rest of their lives? There's evidence available through the American Stroke Association, the American Heart Association,[22] and several other extremely reputable sources that suggests that getting tPA into the right patients quickly enough can substantially reduce their lifelong downstream healthcare costs. Every 15 minutes of time saved can mean an additional 5 percent of stroke patients being discharged to home as opposed to a rehab or skilled nursing facility. So if you can transform a disabling stroke into a nondisabling stroke, meaning that instead of going to a skilled nursing facility, the patient goes home, how many patients do you think we need to save in a year for our program to be considered a success?

"And that doesn't even factor into the calculation each patient's ability to go back to work, pay taxes, or even avoid having a family member have to quit a job to become a homebound caregiver. Then there's the patient's quality of life and everything that goes into it. How can that even be quantified?"

As Dr. Rasmussen's points demonstrate, the challenges inherent in developing and then introducing new healthcare services are not limited to purely technical considerations. Finance, politics, market forces, prestige, professional aspirations, reputational investments, practice precedents, and personal preferences are all, for better or for worse, component pieces in any decision that affects the delivery of healthcare and its associated services. In a word, *people* are a big—if not always acknowledged—part of the equation.

It's a fact that Stacey Winners, the program manager who helped build and implement the Mobile Stroke Treatment Unit program, knows quite well. "We understood," she says, "that to succeed, the Mobile Stroke Treatment Unit needed to work in partnership with local municipalities and Emergency

Medical Service (EMS) systems that are already in place. In the hospital setting, we have a specialized team that has the expertise in treating this type of emergency. We just needed to figure out a way to bring that expertise to individuals outside of the hospital. To do this, we needed to devise a way to access the patient more quickly—even if it was just 15 minutes faster than the traditional method of treating a stroke patient in the emergency room. Those 15 minutes have the potential to be life-changing. And we realized that the only way to do it was to become fully integrated in the city's 911 system. Now, when a 911 call is identified by an emergency medical dispatcher as a potential stroke victim, the package of resources that gets dispatched includes a local EMS squad and the Mobile Stroke Treatment Unit. Both units will arrive within minutes of one another and will work collaboratively to do what's best for the patient.

"On-scene, local EMS perform their initial Cincinnati Pre-Hospital Scale assessment. If they get a result that indicates that they could be dealing with a patient having a stroke, they put the patient right into our squad, where we immediately start our 'stroke alert' process, just as if we were in the emergency department of a hospital. While the team begins to assess the patient and gather a medical history, they will simultaneously place the patient on a cardiac monitor to obtain vital signs, draw blood specimens and process them, and they'll get a CT scan. These images are immediately transmitted to a neuroradiologist and stroke specialist for viewing. Via the portable Telestroke system, our physician determines the best course of treatment for the patient. If the assessment indicates that the patient is experiencing an ischemic stroke, he or she may be eligible for intravenous tPA. If the CT indicates a hemorrhagic stroke, then we can also initiate other medications to start combatting the hemorrhage. We carry all the emergency neuro drugs, as well as advanced cardiac lifesaving drugs. We have a ventilator, a full array of lab equipment, and a CT scanner—so basically we're an emergency room, or hospital, on wheels. One of our program goals is to keep the patients within their healthcare network, so we always ask the patients where they normally receive their care. Based on the severity of their condition and the resources they need, we make every attempt to transport them to that hospital facility.

"But even with all that, we've still had to prove ourselves, particularly with the advocates of rapid EMS transport. There were local squads who said, 'We can get the patient to the hospital within minutes, while you guys sit on scene for half an hour.' This gave us the opportunity to explain that, while it's true that a local squad can get the patient through a hospital's front door really fast, that's not the end of the situation for the patient. It's not an EMS problem. There are potential places that can slow a patient's treatment progress once the patient arrives at the hospital, because when patients enter a healthcare system, they have to be registered and triaged. But what happens if all the ED beds are full, or you only have one physician on staff who's busy with another critical patient?

"With stroke, minutes count, and treatment almost always relies on that CT scan. In the hospital setting, many of the necessary resources that are needed to guide the treatment decisions of stroke can be already in use caring for other critical patients. With our Mobile Stroke Unit, our CT scanner is always open. Our lab is always open. Our physician is always ready for you. You have a team of caregivers concentrating on only you. There are no distractions. You're first in line and our number one priority.

"So, to help the local EMS and fire personnel get a better understanding of what we do, we invite them to watch us work. After just a few minutes of watching the workflow process in the Mobile Stroke Treatment Unit, they gain a true understanding of what our unit is all about. They may not always get to see the process in its entirety, but the next time our paths cross, we always let them know how it turned out. After all, in our minds, they helped expedite the treatment of that patient, so they're a part of the care team, too."

Pausing, Stacey's expression softens, even as her tone grows more serious. "For the first 10 months," she says, "I rode on the truck every day. I was working 13 or more hours a day, seven days a week for 10 months. I had put in countless hours getting the program up and running, and I needed to see it through. It was important to me to make sure that I was there to assist in any way I possibly could—from offering to carry a bag for EMS to helping extract a patient from his or her home, to just offering emotional support to the patient and family. I was fully invested in the unit and in this concept of care, and I wanted others to also see the benefits of the program.

"At times, I guess I was kind of aggressive, maybe even a little pushy in my interaction with the local squads, kind of like the kid sister who constantly annoys you until you finally let her tag along. But, as I saw it, I was building essential relationships that were important to the success of the program. I just felt that I had to show them that I wasn't there to try to take anyone's job. I was there to work alongside them, to work with them to offer the best possible treatment for our patients. Today, whether I'm walking through an ED, passing an ambulance bay, or picking up a shift on the truck, the local EMS and fire crews will stop and say, 'Hey, it's the stroke girl. How's the stroke truck doing?' It doesn't matter if they don't remember my name. All that matters is that they recognize the program and the importance of the concept of providing care in the prehospital setting. And you know, when it's all said and done, that's what really matters. And it feels pretty great."

Dr. Rasmussen's final observations take the core Distance Health concept beyond today's nascent forays into connectivity-supported medical service delivery by imagining some really exciting new places in the emerging cyber-care practice environment. Connected as he is by temperament and the technology-rich nature of the kind of medicine he practices, he sees technology very much as an extension of himself, promising him and his colleagues the opportunity to positively impact the lives of more patients, more quickly, and better than ever before. For him, conducting a face-to-face visit with a patient through a high-definition Internet connection is just a given; it's logical.

"It's what I do," he says. "Seeing and speaking to my patients are critical aspects of my role and my responsibility as a physician. I want my patients to see me and to trust me. I want us to look each other in the eye. I want them to hear my voice so they can feel my sincerity and my concern. I want them to see my empathy and my commitment. There's no replacement for that kind of interaction. And I do it all the time. To me, it's really simple.

"But going forward, now that's when things can start getting really interesting. It's when we start imagining the big stuff, like the long-term management of whole patient populations, particularly patients who have chronic diseases, that you start getting a sense of where we're going. For example, instead of having patients who have high blood pressure visit their doctors every week or two to have a nurse take a BP reading for the purposes of medication adjustment, how about, instead, if they just went on Amazon and bought an FDA-approved digital blood pressure cuff that could communicate with their smartphones? Then their phones could download a log of their readings at regular intervals straight into their doctors' electronic health record systems, which could automatically calculate and track a series of trend lines that would only trigger a notification to the clinician when a patient's numbers started trending in a direction that required a call right now.

"And as we add more devices, we'll find more sophisticated ways to manage a whole range of chronic diseases. Like with digital glucometers for diabetes, or activity monitors for patients with movement disorders. You know, right now we're working on a management plan to help control a patient's Parkinson's disease that uses a smartphone tremor app that was developed by Dr. Jay Alberts in our Department of Bioengineering. All patients have to do is download the app onto a smartphone. And then, when they hold the phone in their hand, the app can measure the intensity, strength, and frequency of their tremors and deliver the results as objective data, which is data that goes straight from the device into the EHR without human intervention, where it will help a physician really understand how effectively the tremor is being managed, not just when the patient comes into the office for a visit, but all the time.

"In that kind of model, instead of a patient visiting a physician every three months, we'll be able to combine a set of digital tools, smartphone apps, decision support algorithms, and video visits in a way that will allow us to fine-tune a patient's medication every week so we can get that patient to his or her best possible point faster, more conveniently, and without the need to travel back and forth a hundred times. I think that's very much where medicine is going. I believe that soon, patients will surround themselves with connected medical devices, way beyond how it was when we were growing up and your house had a thermometer and a scale. Now people are adding blood pressure cuffs and glucometers; even things like pill meters and inhalers are becoming more mainstream. If we use these devices right, if clinicians get involved and offer their patients real guidance, then I think this kind of connectivity will have a real transformative impact on how medicine is practiced.

"But physician involvement is the key. Access alone to lots of different devices, just like access to lots and lots of information from lots of different sources without an expert to help guide you through, has the capacity to cause confusion and, potentially, harm. It's the Internet's power to bring patients and providers together more closely and more frequently that I see as that event horizon over which a totally new kind of patient/doctor relationship will be found. But doctors and nurses, pharmacists, and the whole range of allied health professionals need to understand that, while the Internet is an opportunity to extend the reach of their skills, to do the most good, we all have to get involved so that we can do it right."

A New Clinical Space

As I hope is becoming clear from our glimpse into the world that Dr. Katzan, Karen Jensen, Stacy Winners, and all the other clinical and technology innovators who support their work are doing to forge a truly new cyber-care practice space, what we are witnessing right now is the emergence of a confluence point between medicine and technology that makes Dr. Rasmussen's use of the phrase "event horizon" feel particularly insightful. Commonly associated with black holes in space, an event horizon is generally described as the point where the velocity required to resist the gravitational pull of an object equals the speed of light, meaning that no physical object can attain it, and therefore no object can escape. It's the point of no return, where the gravity generated by something really big is so strong that nothing can resist it.[23]

As we have seen so far, some of the core social and interpersonal relationship structures that we use and reuse to construct our various functional groups are virtually identical to the way the Internet is organized to work. We've also seen how that same connectivity modality, as reflected in the deployment of Cleveland Clinic's single technology infrastructure, can significantly impact a large organization's ability to work as a single enterprise while helping the people involved feel as if they are connected to, and therefore are an active part, of a team that has a real sense of identity and purpose. And, finally, we've been introduced to some forward-thinking programs that are beginning to leverage the real-time connectivity our era's wireless digital halo makes possible to eliminate distance as a parameter in a new kind of cyber-care space where patients and providers can meet and interact at the speed of need.

It is at that transom, that event horizon, between using Internet-based connectivity to connect people to one another so that they can conduct what are still, essentially, slightly modified versions of familiar, real-world activities, and taking the next and inevitable step of creating and fully entering an Internet-based cyber-care space that is its own health-care environment—with its own rules and possibilities, its own potential and problems, and its own tangible sense of place—that we all, patients and providers, find ourselves in the present moment. It can feel a little foreboding, because the enormous *thing* exerting that gravitational force that seems to be pulling us so irresistibly toward itself remains unfinished and unexplored. It is big. It is powerful. And it is still, at least for the moment, composed almost exclusively of potential energy. We haven't crossed that line yet, but we can definitely see it. We're standing on it.

If we are going to make the potential energy of the Internet a power source for the real practice of medicine, we are going to need to imagine and eventually build what I call an Internet of Healthcare. To navigate the Internet of Healthcare, we will need a universal browser that will be capable of doing a wide range of work, such as simple data capture, clinical decision support, caregiver communication, advanced collation, summation and real-time presentation of literature-based treatment information at the bedside, and much, much more. And while the Internet of Healthcare may still remain very much an exercise in speculative imagination, its universal browser is actually already here.

It is still in an early stage of development, but it is misnamed because, while today we may call it an electronic health record, being a *record* is only one small part of what it will ultimately become.

SUMMARY

1. Bringing the right patient and the right clinician together through a technology-supported service is an increasingly important competency in the contemporary practice of medicine. To successfully accomplish these kinds of enhanced clinical services, we must begin with a careful examination of the current practice workflow, carefully mapping each iterative step to a corresponding technology solution. But a first-step gap analysis can never be used as the wireframe blueprint for a finalized service because inherent in the structure of any integrated technology system is the potential to accomplish much more than can be identified within a process that limits itself to simply reproducing a paper-based workflow in a series of computer clicks.

2. Compared to only a decade ago, the general public is far more comfortable with online activities than many healthcare providers may realize. They are already purchasing and beginning to use a wide range of digital medical devices, most of which come with no oversight or guidance from a medical professional. As consumers surround themselves with more and more sophisticated digital health equipment, healthcare providers have a real opportunity to contribute to their safe use, as well as to the creation of a cyber-care practice space in which such devices will play an increasingly important role as the constantly streaming conduit of biometric and other condition-specific patient data and information.

FIGURE 3.3 The Integrated Technology Services Value Equation (continued)

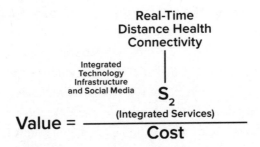

$$\text{Value} = \frac{\substack{\text{Real-Time} \\ \text{Distance Health} \\ \text{Connectivity}}\;\Big|\;\mathbf{S_2}}{\text{Cost}}$$

The second major functional category of Integrated Technology Services allows providers and patients to overcome the boundaries and limitations of physical proximity as a barrier to care, extending the parameters and definition of a medical practice space.

Bottom Line

We are at a transition point between using technology tools to do traditional things better and a cyber-care practice space in which it will be possible to do things that are entirely new and unique. To make the Internet of Healthcare work for all, everyone must participate. Clinicians have a particularly important role to play as the expert arbiters who will ensure that the good a technology can contribute is not supplanted by the potential harm that can result from using healthcare-related information and devices without the proper expert guidance or direction.

Electronic Health Record: Functionality, Adoption, Future

A Night in the Bunker

In 1889, Canadian-born physician Sir William Osler became the first physician-in-chief of the new Johns Hopkins Hospital in Baltimore, Maryland.[1] He was often called "the father of modern medicine."[2] Bedside teaching was so much a part of his style of clinician training[3] that he is sometimes credited with coining the word *rounding*. The story is hard to verify, but it sounds really good, particularly if you are a resident in training hearing it for the first time from one of the staff. During Sir William's tenure, the famous Johns Hopkins dome was still a part of the hospital, so when he guided his team of young physicians from patient to patient, they followed the circular hospital hallway all the way around the base of the dome. Because there were multiple members of the team, they were said to be making their "rounds."

Whether the story is true or not, making rounds is an established and important part of any clinician's life in a hospital setting, contributing to care team cohesion, an improved teamwork dynamic across disciplines (particularly when nurses are included), and more concise communication.[4] Also, it's just a good idea to keep an eye on your patients, especially the ones who are really sick, such as those in an intensive care unit (ICU).

It was a fairly large ICU patient population that Jorge Guzman, MD, was watching over on a cold February night in 2014. Though he presently serves as the vice president of Cleveland Clinic's Regional Medical Operations, on this particular evening he was, as director of Cleveland Clinic's Medical Intensive Care Unit, performing the duties of a critical care clinician who specializes in acute lung injury, acute respiratory distress syndrome, and sepsis. The ICU patient population that was under his watchful eye numbered 78, and they were located in four different hospitals, separated by as much as 45 miles. Instead of rounding on them all, he decided that, for his eleven o'clock rounds, he would only look in on the 12 who needed his closest attention, starting with a gentleman who, though not a "red box," had arrived within the past hour.

"Are we ready?" Dr. Guzman asked, and the two nurses who occupied the workstations located to his right and left stepped in closer to where he was standing at the center of Cleveland Clinic's eHospital technology array, which was located on the anesthesia floor of the main campus's P Building, in a room known as the bunker.

Inside, there were three large tables arranged end-to-end, positioned against the left wall, running lengthwise from the door. The tables were sophisticated devices that could be raised or lowered with the touch of a button. Each supported an identical arrangement of five flat-screen monitors: one large one on the left, by itself, and four smaller ones arranged in a square, two across, two down, to the right. Each

FIGURE 4.1 eHospital Intensive Care Unit Monitoring Center

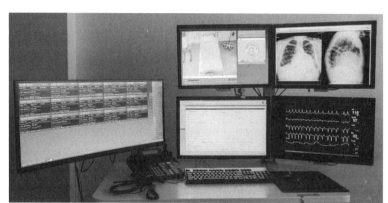

A deceptively simple-looking technology array that allows critical care specialists to monitor patients in multiple locations with data visualization that maximizes attention and focus while minimizing unproductive visual processing and on-screen clutter.

workstation had a keyboard, a mouse, and a telephone (Figure 4.1). On the white wall behind the stations was a Cleveland Clinic "Patients First" circular logo, painted in blue, green, and black.

Over the center set of screens there was a high-definition digital camera mounted at about eye level, small, unobtrusive, but still definitely in view. Each workstation also had a rolling chair that, more often than not, ended up pushed to one side because ICU monitoring personnel tended to stand at their stations.

It wasn't until you visited the space at night, when the unit was live between seven o'clock in the evening and seven o'clock in the morning, that its nickname made sense. With the faces of the doctor and nurses lit only by glowing monitor screens that turned eyeglasses into mirrors and thoughtful concentration into stony, shadowed stares, it was almost impossible to imagine calling the place anything *other* than the bunker.

On the big monitor to Dr. Guzman's left were 12 "tiles" displayed in three rows. Each tile had a bright red header across the top with a patient's name and location. Each tile also displayed the patient's vital signs, including temperature, pulse, blood pressure, respiratory rate, and SpO2 (which is the amount of oxygenated hemoglobin in the blood),[5] as continuously updated trend graphs. On the far right-hand side of the large screen was a column with a scrollable list of the names, locations, and present physiological color statuses of all 78 ICU patients, with the "red boxes" at the top and the "green boxes" underneath.

He was looking at a lot of information about the sickest patients in four of Cleveland Clinic's regional hospitals. But with just a glance, he knew which patients needed the most attention, who they were, where they were, and why they were having difficulty. It was all right there. If a patient got into real trouble, his or her tile would shake and a bell would ring. You couldn't miss it.

The work that had gone into building the eHospital display, tying everything directly into the MyPractice electronic health record system so that all the device data generated by the various monitoring equipment could be constantly displayed as simple lines trending on a graph, the work that made it possible for the actual EHR, with all of its connectivity capabilities, associated images—x-rays, echoes, photographs, etc.—to be displayed right there, next to a screen upon which the images generated by a controllable high-definition digital camera feed that came directly from each ICU bed could be seen; it was all really remarkable. But it was the data visualization aspect that was, to him, the stroke of real inspiration.

At a glance, he could do what amounted to a rapid visual triage of the hospital system's sickest patients, risk-stratified based on real-time device data coming off the monitors that was continually being analyzed by rules and algorithms that had been written in partnership with Quantitative Health Sciences, and generated dynamic predictive models based on agreed-upon parameters of statistical probability.

It would take him longer to describe what he was doing when he looked at the screen than it did to actually do it. Which was a real trick, especially when you looked at the data from which the visualizations were being generated. It was all there, in the EHR. You could pull up the data tables, with their columns and lines and hundreds of little black numbers, peppered throughout with little red numbers that looked more scattered than they did important. It was just data. But visualized onscreen, it was *information*.

The top name on the green box list was new because the 58-year-old man had only just arrived in this regional hospital's ICU because the symptoms of his congestive obstructive pulmonary disease (COPD)—shortness of breath, quantity and color of phlegm, etc.—had suddenly gotten worse. The condition could have been triggered by an infection or exposure to something environmental, and it would probably last for several days. It had to be taken seriously because it was associated with a serious chronic disorder of the heart.

Dr. Guzman double-clicked the patient's name, and the screens before him instantly filled with the patient's EHR summary page, a full-screen vitals display (identical to the screen that was blinking next to the patient's bed, which was a 50-minute drive from the bunker), and a chest x-ray. With a second double-click, he activated the camera in the patient's room. The "doorbell" notice made the nurse, the patient, and his daughter, who was sitting next to the bed, all turn to face the camera.

Activating his own camera, Dr. Guzman took control of the TV mounted near the ceiling in one corner of the ICU upon which he could now be seen. Smiling, he said, "Hello, I'm Dr. Jorge Guzman. I just wanted to let you know that my team and I are here if you need anything tonight."

"That's all right," the nurse said. "We don't need anything. But thank you."

She was about to turn the camera off when her patient said, "Who is that?"

Dr. Guzman introduced himself again quickly because he had encountered this nurse before. She was one of several nurses and other staff across the health system who felt that the eHospital "eyes in the sky," as some called it, were intrusive and offensive. They didn't see why they needed someone looking over their shoulders and second-guessing their work. Dr. Guzman did not take it personally. He understood why the eHospital team could be seen as Big Brother.

But that was not the program's intent. Far from it. The program was meant to support the on-site staff in a way that they had never been supported before. Before eHospital, any regional hospital ICU patient showing signs of distress immediately became a candidate for transfer to the main campus, which was disruptive for the patient and for the staffs at two hospitals. It was also expensive. With the remote monitoring service in place, there was an experienced critical care team virtually stationed right alongside the local ICU team and, together, they could address a much wider range of situations on-site. That was the idea, and so far it was working.

It was working so well, in fact, that one of the first things the eHospital team had done was to remove their equipment from the ICUs on the main campus because, as it turned out, they were just increasing cost without adding value to the most intensely staffed and managed ICUs in the health system. In the regional hospitals, which normally treated lower acuity patients and therefore did not have the same level of physician staffing, the service did add value by supporting the on-site staff with specialty expertise exactly when it was needed. It would just take a little time for the staff to adjust.

"So where are you?" the patient asked as his daughter stood up and stared at the television.

"I'm on Cleveland Clinic's main campus downtown. I'm here with two specially trained nurses, and we're available any time anyone needs us. We just wanted to say hello."

"You can see us?" the daughter asked.

"Yes. We have special equipment that connects us to everything that's going on. We can see all of the information coming from your monitoring devices, and we can see you through the camera."

"That's really something," the patient said. "I've never seen anything like that."

"Yes, well, that's fine," the nurse said, stepping over to pull the blanket up over the patient's chest. "Now it's time to get some sleep. Thank you."

"Well, she was pleasant," the nurse standing to Dr. Guzman's right said as the image of the ICU disappeared from the screen.

"One friend at a time," Dr. Guzman said. "We'll get there."

Four hours later, at three in the morning, the patient went red box, and his box shook as the warning bell dinged. Almost immediately there came a request buzzer from the nurse, and within seconds, Dr. Guzman and his team were back online. The patient was in distress. He was experiencing significant shortness of breath, his heart rate was up, as was his blood pressure, and the residents on-site needed support. Most immediate was the question of whether the patient needed to be intubated, a procedure that would insert a breathing tube through his mouth and down his throat.

"No," Dr. Guzman said, wanting to avoid intubation and the associated invasiveness of the procedure for the patient.

Instead, he guided the residents through a medical and physical intervention that combined a short-acting, inhaled bronchodilator medication, a pain medication, some very specific physical repositioning of the patient using a partial backboard and pillows, and a tightly fitted oxygen delivery device that would help de-constrict his airway. Within minutes the patient was breathing more easily, and Dr. Guzman and his team could see that his vitals were dropping back into the normal range.

The nurse thanked the team, and Dr. Guzman probably would not have thought anything else of it except that, right before he was about to end his shift the next morning, the same nurse buzzed, asking that he turn on the camera and take control of the TV. Glancing at his nursing team, he did as he was asked, wondering what was up. It didn't seem as if the patient was in any kind of trouble. They could see his vitals, and everything looked fine. So why would the nurse be asking for a conference?

When the camera came on, Dr. Guzman found the patient, his daughter, and the nurse smiling and waving hello. In a somewhat hoarse voice, the patient said, "I just wanted to say thank you to you guys. For what you did for me last night. That was scary. I didn't want a tube . . . so . . . just . . . you know . . ."

"Thank you for what you did for my dad," his daughter said, putting her hand on her father's shoulder. "We're glad you were watching."

"Yeah," the nurse agreed. "We're glad you were watching."

From Paper to Clicks to . . . Paper?

The eHospital system is based on a far more extensive use of the MyPractice electronic health record's functional capabilities than any of the other clinical services we've discussed.

eHospital's power comes from the way all the monitoring equipment around an ICU bed is able to feed real-time data directly into the EHR, where it is captured as device data before being validated and permanently recorded. The algorithms that create the trend lines and various predictive modeling visualizations delivered through the eHospital technology array were built to interact directly with data in the EHR, using its quantitative management capabilities to accomplish real-time, dynamic tasks that feel totally at odds with the name of the system upon which it is built, the electronic health record.

It's the *record* part that may feel a bit out of place here because, increasingly, it is. To understand why, let's start with a very brief look at the history of that now-ubiquitous device, the mobile phone.

Believe it or not, the first patent for a "wireless" phone was issued in 1908, but it was not until the 1940s that engineers at AT&T got a functional version of a mobile phone working around what they called "base stations," which were kind of like the first cell towers, allowing taxi drivers and emergency services personnel to use what were really two-way radios to improve how they did their jobs.[6] In 1983, Motorola introduced the first generation of what we might call a true mobile phone with the Motorola DynaTAC 800X, which, at 13 inches in length, was almost immediately nicknamed the "brick."[7] The brick worked great for its time, though it was not really something customers carried around. Instead the term "car phone" caught on because it was your car that gave your mobile phone its mobility (unless of course you went with the very stylish shoulder strap–equipped carrying case, which was about as big as your average toaster oven).

The second generation of mobile phones was released in the early 1990s when mobile networks began using digital circuit switching in their transmissions, expanding the range of mobile phone coverage. At the same time, advances in microchip technology were allowing phones to be made small enough to be carried in a pocket or a purse. The third generation of mobile phones, or 3G, were the first more-than-a-phone phones that could do more than just transmit and receive the human voice,[8] which led to the 4G speed and data capacity of today's wireless technology that Dr. Rasmussen cited as the foundational requirement for the reliable, real-time video connectivity that makes our various remote stroke services possible.

Probably the best-known example of the more-than-a-phone mobile phone is the Apple iPhone, first introduced by Steve Jobs on January 9, 2007[9]—though, a full eight years earlier, in 1999, Research in Motion (RIM) had unveiled its first BlackBerry branded device,[10] giving "business" people access to their e-mail and calendars, in addition to being an actual phone.

Remember the "CrackBerry"? Oh, how quickly we forget.

The real mobile phone, as we use it today, only got its start sometime in the mid-2000s. I didn't trace the history of the mobile phone over time to make the point that, once they hit a critical developmental transition matrix, telephones changed quickly—though they did. Instead, think about yourself and your use of your "smartphone," a term that first appeared in print in 1995 to describe AT&T's "PhoneWriter Communicator"[11] (which could receive and make cellular calls, as well as send and receive faxes, e-mails, and pages).[12] How long did it take you to figure out how to use the first smartphone you ever owned? How long did it take you to get comfortable using the smartphone you presently own? More important, how long was it before you started wishing that your device could do more than it does?

What? I can only take pictures, not videos? What? I can't see the person I'm talking to in real time on the screen? Oh,

I can? OK. But what about counting how many steps I take during the day? Or telling me instantly where I can get the best pizza within five minutes' walking distance of my present location as determined by a Global Positioning System satellite?

A satellite! for Pete's sake.

The adoption of technology can have incredibly physical ramifications, but the changes happen in ways that are sometimes all but invisible because they involve redirecting so much of our attention to the new things that the old just cease to exist, both from the physical landscape and from our internal mental landscape as well. This redirection of our attention, combined with an almost simultaneous kind of amnesia about the reality of the world as it previously existed, can result in an oddly unsettling sense of time-focused frustration.

It seems as if, in our contemporary lives, we want the next new technology-based thing at exactly the same instant that we are introduced to the latest new technology-based thing. It's like "new" now means "old" because the time that something spends being new has been so drastically contracted as to become virtually immeasurable.

And that's what's happening with today's electronic health record. We call it a *record*, but, looking back, it was probably all but inevitable that the clinicians using it would immediately want it to do more than it was originally designed to do because, like the other technologies we were just talking about, it was obvious that it *could* do more. Even its core structure or format was a source of dissatisfaction almost from the very start, even though it was based on a model that every physician knows well: the paper medical chart. Which, by the way, *is* a record because it is static and lives in a single place, alone, until it is retrieved and used again, usually by one user at a time, serving as a repository of history and nothing more, other than, perhaps, the documented evidence of a physician's thought process.

An electronic health record is not static, and it is not limited to any single user at any single time. Though, as William Morris, MD, associate chief information officer of Cleveland Clinic Technology and Innovation, is quick to point out, this was exactly the model from which the early creators of EHR systems were encouraged to work.

"With the electronic health record," he says, "the words themselves imply a repository of information intended to basically be a chart, which is what we physicians originally said we wanted. As we were moving from a paper to an electronic model, we said that we wanted the experience to feel like the paper experience, and that's what the vendors and developers delivered for us. We took a familiar system and we rerendered it—kind of like the first movies, which were actually just films of plays.

"In those early movies, the audience got an only slightly different version of a very familiar experience. It wasn't until the true pioneers of film began transforming movies by using different perspectives, different camera angles and lenses, leaps in time and space, and all those visual storytelling innovations that were unlike anything you could ever see, or even imagine in the physical performance of a play, that a new and unique art form was born.

"I think that's exactly what's happening in healthcare. There are those who, for some very good reasons, advocate what they call an optimization of the EHR to better reflect the charting style we were taught in medical school. They believe it just takes too many clicks to accomplish what we need to do, and that by reducing the clicks, we will increase the usefulness of the EHR.

"But why should we want to treat patient records as paper? The first question is one of semantics. What are we really talking about? Are we talking about a health *record*? Or are we actually talking about something that's intended to be a system that can turn data into knowledge? Like a virtual practice environment, I envision an electronic health mentor or colleague. I expect this tool not just to be a repository for storing information, but to be something that is fundamentally different. In today's EHRs, we have pages and pages of content that may have some context, some metadata around it, but it still requires you to actually go in there and interrogate that data before you can pull any knowledge out of it, which is exactly how it was done on paper.

"For me, it's a fundamental question: can we imagine a kind of electronic health practice partner in which each interaction with the data will actually improve the fidelity of the information itself? If the answer is yes, then how can we take what we have, which is basically an electronic version of a paper world, and make it do what we know it can do, make it become what we know it can become?"

As we are about to see, the answer to Dr. Morris's question will most likely be found at the confluence point where the clinicians themselves, the actual stewards of the data contained in the EHR and the very professionals who use the knowledge contained in that data to accomplish their work, become personally engaged in the trajectory of the system's development.

If It's Just Like What I've Got,
Why Should I Change?

The man who is usually credited with the idea of "computerizing" medical records is Lawrence L. Weed, MD, who, in the mid-1960s, described some of the ways he imagined that computers could be used to reorganize medical information in a way that would increase efficiency and positively impact the delivery of care.[13] His concepts proved so appealing that they inspired a University of Vermont project called PROMIS (Problem-Oriented Medical Information System), which began in 1967 and led to the problem-oriented medical record (POMR) that was first used in the Medical Center Hospital of Vermont in 1970.[14]

Designed to organize a patient's record around a medical problem, with all diagnostic and therapeutic activities linked to that problem, the problem-oriented medical record was an early and influential attempt to imbue computerized record-keeping with a cohesive internal structure. By associating charges to the items on the problem list, a computerized problem-oriented medical record could generate a detailed list of charges that more accurately reflected everything that had occurred during a patient's treatment,[15] clearly illustrating the very tight link between clinical activities and billing processes that were written into the technology from its very beginning.

Opinions about how effective the computerized medical record systems actually were centered on a core conflict— that of entering information into the system as discrete data, which is data that can be searched and collated (as in, select from this list and click the appropriate box), against capturing a narrative, or free text description of a patient's situation that places context around a clinician's thoughts and treatment approach but that makes it virtually impossible to search or sort.

To be useful on a larger scale, information must be entered discretely, but to be useful at the level of direct patient care, the medical record needs to tell the patient's personal health story.

It is a dichotomy that has yet to be satisfactorily resolved, if it ever will be. And it is representative of much of the electronic health record's somewhat bumpy developmental path.

From its earliest incarnations to the present day, the EHR has been a focus of both creative optimism about all the new things it will allow clinicians and clinician scientists to do, and real-world frustrations that are most often expressed in two fundamental user complaints: (1) it takes too long to do what I want to do; and (2) there is so much information in here that I can't find anything.

A fair and thoughtful discussion of the appropriate methodology for effective data capture and management, and its required supporting computational architecture, let alone the human/machine interface components that are most effective in eliminating confusion and maximizing efficiency as measured by time to comprehension and informed action, is beyond the scope of this book, as is a review of the inherent strengths and weaknesses of different EHR systems developed by technology vendors or some healthcare provider systems themselves. What is germane to this story is our experience in rolling out a single, integrated EHR system in Cleveland Clinic's large group physician practice, the challenges and successes we experienced along the way, and the direction in which our physicians and their IT partners are now taking our EHR in order to make it as useful as possible in the future.

It is difficult to imagine a more invasive initiative than telling every one of our physicians that they were going to be expected to change a part of their professional workflow as fundamental and personal as patient care charting. But in 2001 that is exactly what we did. It was a project that, much like the EHR itself, was filled with promise and packed tight with hair-triggered ignition points. It is a testament to the professionalism and dedication of our staff that, years before anyone even imagined a federal EHR reimbursement program or a single meaningful use regulation, we successfully undertook and completed an enterprise-wide integrated EHR go-live.

This is not to say that we didn't face our share of problems, the first of which came in the form of a (very reasonable) question some of our clinicians asked at the same moment we were taking our first tentative steps forward: if all an electronic medical record does is put information in the computer instead of on a paper chart, and I have to take the time to learn how to use this thing, which is going to slow me down in my clinic, affect my efficiency, my productivity, and ultimately my ability to concentrate on taking care of my patients, then why in the world would I ever want to do it?

It's a question that we are still answering today, and it leads us back to our original vision of the EHR's eventual transition from being solely a record to fulfilling the role many physicians and nurses would like to see it achieve: becoming a true healthcare resource capable of supporting a clinician's practice-specific tasks *and* real-time decision-making activities.

You Have to Start Somewhere, So Why Not Start with a Champion?

Our EHR journey began with registration and scheduling in our outpatient clinics, moving to full functionality in all internal medicine practices in our Family Health Centers and then to our specialty clinics, before ending with our inpatient practice as its own project, first on the main campus, and then in our system hospitals. The entire initiative took almost five years to complete, and it involved hundreds, if not thousands, of IT support personnel, end-user trainers, curriculum creators, writers, graphic designers, nurses, administrators, and what we came to call our physician champions.

The idea of the physician champion arose early, and for what, in hindsight, should have been a very obvious reason. The true thrust of the project was not just persuading someone to grudgingly turn a computer on in the exam room, but to encourage our clinicians to adopt and really use the EHR as a functional part of a new, technology-enabled practice model, so our clinicians were the central focus of our attention. As a physician group practice, Cleveland Clinic is a physician-run organization, meaning that decisions regarding changes that will impact patient safety and care quality are always made by those who are actually responsible for doing the work.

With that structure in mind, we identified an initial group of internal medicine physicians who also had a special interest in healthcare informatics to create, coordinate, and communicate the details of what we called at the time the Epic rollout project. As physicians with experience managing chronic disease populations, these clinicians had a very data-driven approach and, as founding members of our Physician Advisory Group (PAG), they also had a direct connection to the opinions and experiences of their physician colleagues, which resulted in a rollout project that made communication one of its top priorities.

Tirelessly, they hosted "lunch and learns," and "brown bag" seminars held at times and in locations that would be convenient for their targeted clinician audiences. They made seemingly endless PowerPoint presentations, conducted clinical rounds, spoke to any gathering of two or more physicians or nurses who would hold still, and were supported by a new, if modest, strategic communication team that created electronic and paper newsletters, FAQs, quick reference guides, wallet cards, and everything else they could think of that would catch a clinician's attention long enough to make an educational point, including branded intranet websites and little gold eCleveland Clinic lapel pins for anyone who completed our EHR classroom training session.

They emphasized the connectivity aspects of the system, demonstrated how the data entered into it became a clinical resource that could be shared by a patient's entire care team—which was a real positive given the multidisciplinary nature of our practice—and made themselves available, individually and as teams, anytime, anywhere to do personal training sessions, answer questions, and hear ideas that might make the system more attractive to the physicians it was intended to support. They also pushed early and hard for the adoption of the MyChart secure patient portal feature that the Epic system enabled, talking about patient empowerment and a closer relationship between patients and their providers at clinician-oriented events, continuing medical education (CME) seminars, and in as many Cleveland Clinic community "Health Talks" as they could possibly attend.

But there was one hurdle that this revolving team of early clinical supporters simply could not overcome. Because they were working on what most of their physician colleagues saw as an IT project, meaning that they had, in varying degrees of time allocation, additional responsibilities that prevented them from practicing full-time in their clinics, they could be dismissed by those physicians who were inclined to do so as not being "one of them."

"Sure," they would counter, often in front of a group. "You only practice a couple days a week, so you have plenty of time to learn this stuff—setting up your 'smart phrases' and figuring out your keystrokes and shortcuts. I've got a full schedule of patients waiting for me right now. I don't have time for this."

It was a tough contention, on its face, to refute. But it led us to our breakthrough concept of the physician champion.

The physician champion is a professional personification of the "like attracts like" idea that says that human beings tend to be attracted to other people who are like themselves.[16] It is by no means a law of nature, but it is a common enough notion, and it makes a certain amount of sense. We gravitate toward others who, in some way, remind us of ourselves because we are comfortable with the familiar, and we find shared experiences and interests to be good foundational material with which to build relationships.

So when we discovered that there were physicians who took to the EHR particularly well, who attended the classroom training we provided and then availed themselves of the on-site training support we made available during the first week of a departmental go-live, and who then proceeded to use the technology in ways that, in fact, made their practices work better, we, at first, very politely asked them how they had done it. And then, even more politely, we asked if they wouldn't mind telling their colleagues how they could do it, too. To our surprise and delight, many did, establishing a direct physician connection between the technology and the group practice and changing the entire dynamic of the conversation and program.

Suddenly, it became a really positive time. After the initial logistical nightmare of planning and then executing an implementation, system testing, end-user training, go-live, follow-up, and troubleshooting initiative of this size, complexity, and interpersonal magnitude, and especially after we discovered that there were sincere and enthusiastic clinicians who embraced our new technology tools not because of our persuasive efforts, but because they actually delivered the kind of value we had long believed they would, success felt really good.

We took a lot of "before and after" pictures of physicians' offices, first stacked with charts and cluttered with paper, and then clean and tidy once the EHR did its work. We must have used a thousand different variations of the quote, "I didn't think I would like it, but now that I'm using it, I don't know how I ever got along without it," that we heard so often from our doctors and nurses that, after a while, it became a bit of a cliché. We even made life-sized color cutouts of real MyChart patients holding a sign that said, "I'm an eCleveland Clinic MyChart Patient. Are you?" that we stood up in the lobbies of our Family Health Centers to promote the availability of the new service.

Most important, we were able to finally begin answering the "If it's just like a paper chart, why should I bother using it?" question that was among the first we encountered at the outset of the project.

We answered that question by pointing out that the data captured in the electronic health record was now accessible to any clinician who needed it, anytime, anywhere there was a computer connected to the Internet. And how, after only a couple of years, our master patient index already contained the records of millions of patients, many of whom were signing up for MyChart as a way of staying connected to the activities related to their care and to their Cleveland Clinic providers of choice.

We initiated DrConnect, a service through which physicians who referred their patients to Cleveland Clinic for specialty care could see the material documented by the treating physicians through a secure online portal. Once patients answered yes to the question, "Would you like your physician at home to have access to the medical record your doctors create about you while you're here?" their referring physicians received an e-mail asking them to log into their DrConnect account to view the secure information it contained. At a stroke, communicating with the physicians who entrusted their patients to our specialists was liberated from the whims of the U.S. mail–delivered discharge notice; and every referring physician who signed up for the service became one of our virtual clinician partners.

None of which would have been possible without our newly branded MyPractice EHR.

Addressing questions about security, we pointed out that every action conducted within our EHR was logged and recorded, meaning that we always knew who was accessing what data and for what purpose, a promise that is impossible to make with a paper chart. When left unattended, who knows who picks up a paper chart and looks at it?

We could show our clinicians that their patients were in fact opening the test results that were released into MyChart, which was something we could not say about results contained in an envelope and mailed.

And eventually we could even begin publishing stories such as the following from our MyChart eNewsletter:

Cleveland Clinic Patient, Deb Sheren, Uses MyChart to Instantly Access Her Medical Records During an Unexpected Hospitalization in Michigan

Cleveland Clinic's MyChart website and mobile application allow patients to securely access portions of their electronic medical records, see test results, message the doctor's office, renew prescriptions, request appointments, and more, anytime, from anywhere. These functionalities provide a number of benefits. For instance, when a patient travels far from home and suddenly requires medical attention, that patient can use MyChart to access their medical information on a computer or a mobile device right at the point of care.

For Deb Sheren, a Cleveland Clinic patient and avid MyChart user, this made all the difference during a recent visit to see her father in Michigan. A few months prior, Deb had been hospitalized and diagnosed with pancreatitis. "My doctors couldn't find a cause at the time," she says, "so they said, 'let's just see how it goes.' A few months went by and my father was hospitalized up in Michigan, so I went to visit him. A few hours after we arrived, I didn't feel so good. Then I started feeling terrible. We called an ambulance and when I was admitted to the hospital I told the ER doctor, 'This happened in January and I think I know what it is.' So she drew blood, ran some tests and confirmed that I had another case of pancreatitis."

After Deb's ER doctor gave her test results to her brother and partner to review, Deb said, "Wait a minute," reaching into her pocket and handing over her smartphone. "I told them to go to the MyChart site, log in, and pull up my test results from January so we could compare the values. When my doctor came back, we handed her the phone and showed her my results."

Because Deb was able to access MyChart on her mobile device, her Cleveland Clinic medical record became immediately available to Deb, her ER doctor and all the other caregivers involved in her treatment.

"Every time a new doctor came in, I'd hand them my phone so they could see what tests had already been run and what the results had been," Deb says. "The Internist that was overseeing my care in Michigan said, 'You know, you probably saved yourself tens of thousands of dollars' worth of tests, because you could show us what tests had already been run and what the results were.' Not only did it save redoing those tests, I probably would have had to stay in the hospital another day or two just to run some of them."

Deb says having her MyChart account easily accessible while in Michigan made her experience of receiving treatment away from home much more comfortable. "It was like I was carrying my medical records right in my pocket. I felt reassured that my doctors weren't going to repeat any of the tests I'd already been given, and that they had a broader history on me than just that one event. I was as new to them as they were to me, but because they were able to view my information in MyChart, they could get a better idea of the state of my health overall."

Once Deb was stable, her Michigan doctors cleared her to return home to Cleveland for any follow-up treatment that was needed. "While I was in the hospital, I used my laptop to log in to Cleveland Clinic's website and search for pancreatitis specialists in my network. I found four doctors that met my criteria. I also used MyChart's secure 'Message My Doctor' feature to send my primary care physician, Dr. Lori Posk, a message. I explained what had happened, gave her the names of the specialists I had found, and asked for her advice. I love that no matter what Cleveland Clinic doctor I need to see, they can pull up all of my information at the point of care. I don't have to re-explain my whole situation, or worry about forgetting something that might be important for my physician to know."

Deb says she'd certainly suggest signing up for a MyChart account to anyone who may be interested. "I like having MyChart because then I have secure access to all my records anytime I want. I feel good knowing that no matter where I may be, another healthcare provider can access my records," she says. "MyChart also gives you the ability to educate yourself about what's going on with your health. I appreciate that I can see normal ranges alongside my test results, so I can look at what my results are measuring, what the normal ranges are, and what might be causing them to be different. MyChart really allows you to become an educated participant in your own healthcare experience."

As we can see, every answer to our original, "so why should I use it?" challenge question flows directly from the availability of an integrated EHR system that our clinicians actually use. Over time, our clinician users have become increasingly involved in how the system works, and the things it is able to do. In 2010 we created the Clinical Systems Office, which is a dedicated group of doctors, nurses, and IT professionals within the IT Division who spend all their time thinking about how the EHR works now and how it can be improved based on the feedback they receive from our Physician Advisory Groups, their interactions with other providers, and their own personal experience.

Because our original strategy demanded that we implement a lot of technology in a very efficient way, much of the work we did over the past 15 years was very linear, regimented, and tightly controlled. We got really good at project management, and our IT teams learned to function very precisely. We have a team of senior IT executives who guided our organization through a logistical tsunami, and they did it with poise and good grace. They showed a lot of heart, and we received many complimentary notes and e-mails about how they brought these enormous projects home against some very aggressive timelines.

What might not have been so apparent to our colleagues not directly involved with these endeavors was that we were also implementing a different kind of organizational structure at the same time that we were putting in all that hardware and training on all that software. We always knew that if our vision of a technology-enabled medical practice model was really going to work, there would come a time when the relationship between the people who "own" the technology and the people who "own" the medical practice would need to change.

We call it our transformation, and we've been working on it for years. It is the final phase of what we see as the beginning of our transformed enterprise, and it centers on the idea of creating a new kind of functional relationship that places

IT professionals and clinical experts together, every day, right inside the practice, experiencing the work, the patients, and the personalities, absorbing the energy of the clinical space and understanding the challenges, goals, and aspirations of the group in a way that would not happen otherwise.

Just as we came to realize that eCleveland Clinic's technology-based services were expressions not of a distinct or separate entity but of Cleveland Clinic's core values, we have understood for a long time that the value of technology, like the value of any tool, is measured not by its cost but by how our people use it. And if the usefulness of our tools is to increase over time, the people who use those tools must be the people who are guiding their development.

To better understand where our technology is headed in the future, the remainder of this chapter features several of our physician leaders who are involved in translating the aspirations and vision of their clinical colleagues directly into our evolving technology infrastructure. It is this kind of collegial effort, this close, personal partnership, and this intimate understanding of what it means to be a practicing clinician that will provide the road map to the future vision described in this book's final chapter.

AMY MERLINO, MD

*Obstetrics and Gynecology,
Cleveland Clinic Women's Health Institute*

Documentation, Communication, and Clinical Coordination

As a physician, I specialize in addressing the complications and issues related to high-risk pregnancies, which means that I see patients in an office setting and in the operating room. It also means that I have a skill set that is very valuable to my colleagues, so their access to me, when they need me, is really essential.

In that very brief description of my own medical practice, I just summarized everything I think is important about electronic health record technology. If we really think about it, has there ever been one single common space that everyone who is involved in patient care actually shares, together? Physically, the answer is no. There are doctors who will never step foot in an OR, and there are doctors who will never see their patients anywhere other than in an ED. There are doctors who only ever practice in their own private offices, and there are doctors who will only read x-rays and other images without ever actually meeting the patients they are examining. We all have our specialties and our special interests. And we all have our own practice space that is exactly right for the work we do. So there has never really been one single space that brings all clinicians together—until now.

Today, the practice space that every member of a patient's care team shares is the electronic health record. The EHR is where we all come together, even if we are located in separate clinical facilities, to document the work we do, to order the services we need, to receive the results that will inform our decisions, and to educate one another about the details of our patient's situation and progress.

That's why I believe it is so important that we also come together and create a standardized view of how we use the EHR that includes how we document, and the etiquette around how we conduct ourselves as healthcare providers inside this new virtual practice environment. For example, on a paper chart, a patient's problem list can function like a clinician's reminder list, recording what the provider thinks may be going on at a particular time. On a paper chart, that provider may refer back to the problem list the next time the patient visits, but managing what's on and what's removed from it isn't much of a priority. In a group practice in which the EHR is a shared resource between multiple doctors and the patient, too, the rules around who adds to a problem list and who takes things off become much more important. It's that kind of physician etiquette that we need to address. And getting to this new way of using technology as a shared clinical location will require physicians, nurses, and other clinicians to be engaged in the future development of our tools and work-flows so that they can be constructed in a way that will resonate with the clinicians who will actually use them.

That's why, as a physician, I originally got involved in clinical informatics: because I could see how key technology was becoming to how we practice. You know, it wasn't so long ago that IT people would just show up and plug in a computer, and then they'd leave the clinicians to use that computer any way they could. Since there wasn't really that much interaction between the clinical side of the practice and the IT people who were supporting it, we were all left pretty much hoping that the systems would function in a way that was right for the work we were trying do.

But now, we've developed what I call the translator concept, which is a new kind of relationship between medical and IT professionals who all live inside the practice and can therefore serve as that point where clinical demands and the realities of a technology build come together. That's the role of clinical informatics as I see it, and it's an exciting way of looking at what we do.

Because the EHR exists, things are changing; and because things are changing, the EHR needs to reflect the best of those changes in ways that will positively impact clinical workflows. That's only going to happen effectively if the people who really understand both disciplines help guide the practice along through smart, informed decisions that reflect the changing realities of a very complex, very important process.

Documentation is a perfect example. Documenting the care a clinician delivers to a patient is more than just a written list of activities. Physician documentation reflects the thought process that moved a clinician through a diagnosis and the formulation of a treatment plan. It's part of how we were trained, and it's part of what actually makes a physician a physician. Without asking the patient subjective questions, without reviewing history, I can't complete my assessment and my plan: I can't do my job.

All physicians have individualized aspects to how they think and how they document, and on a paper chart, stored in a single physician's office or in the repository associated with a defined group of clinicians that doesn't change much over time, those individualized idiosyncrasies can work and, in some cases, add value. But with an EHR, in a practice as large and dynamic as ours, with as many different professionals who touch the system and the data it contains—which I think is a reflection of where all of healthcare is going as health information exchanges emerge to connect hospitals and practices across the country—the shared practice space of the EHR is becoming *our* practice space. To use it most effectively, we're going to have to write some new rules of the road.

When you switch from writing things down on a piece of paper to putting them into a computerized system, you're not simply moving text over from a static template. What you document, such as the history of present illness or review of systems, when you convert those into a digital system, they become a part of the technology. So you must mimic, as much as you can, the thought process of the physicians to give them the right tools to capture information in a way that reflects how they think and work. But that's not always an easy thing to do. For example, in our inpatient setting, our EHR presented the doctors' documentation of their notes in a small part of the screen. But when you transfer the thought process we all learned in medical school, there was a disconnect, because the most important part of the note is the material that is different from everything else in your assessment plan—which appears at the bottom of the note. So there is a technology concept that says that we should just flip the note so that now you're doing the assessment and plan first, making the most important parts more visible on the screen. But that would mean that the subjective/objective portion of the review would come next, which is backward from how the paper chart is put together. Even though our reason for proposing the change was to use the technology to give the clinician better visibility to the most important part of the note, we immediately got a lot of pushback from providers saying, "But I don't think that way!"

That's what I meant about the need for the clinical and the IT team to work together. You have to have that translator, that clinical informatics representative right there as you're working to make the tool work better for providers while making sure that you are guiding your technology vendor to implement improvements that exert the minimum amount of change in order to maintain the maximum amount of efficiency and stability.

The other absolutely critical service our team provides is support, on the ground, ready and able to help our clinicians get accustomed to using the system well. Clinicians are not going to remember every detail of a classroom training session once they are back on the floor, so you need someone who is really skilled at working with the system in a specific clinical setting to be available to your clinicians, right there, at the elbow, when they need them. In the context of the actual practice, these skilled support people can help clinicians solidify some really good habits, and prevent them from falling back on old habits because of time and other pressures.

That speaks directly to the value of the clinical information translator function in medical practice I mentioned earlier. When seen in that light, the view of the entire technology function will change inside the organization. Historically, much of the responsibility for making decisions around what technologies were appropriate for a particular clinical application was left solely to clinicians in the practice. But I would argue that there's a better way, and that is to create a clinical/IT function that is so tightly aligned to the organization that the organization's leadership can confidently start seeing the group as what is essentially their own dedicated consulting vendor.

In this model, clinicians can ask questions of an internal expert resource that, as a team, has a more objective view than, for example, a third-party vendor that has, as its priority, making a sale. This expert resource can help you make more informed decisions based on your needs and the needs of the organization, and also help make sure that, when you do invest in a technology solution, that you are establishing a set of operating standards that will help your clinicians and everyone else use that system to its fullest possible extent.

That's where I see the greatest opportunity for doctors and IT professionals to come together, going forward. We now have this shared virtual practice environment, this emerging cyber-care space that is unique to this moment in our history. We are watching it develop every day. It is our challenge, our privilege, and our responsibility to contribute, as best we can, to making it the best tool it can be. To do that, I believe that we need to create a new kind of healthcare professional relationship, one that brings the practice of medicine and the disciplines of information technology together in a more thoroughly integrated way than ever before. If we do that, which is exactly the work we are pursuing in the Clinical Systems Office, then we might just make a real difference to both our clinical colleagues and the patients we all are here to serve.

It takes real work and a lot of patience. I can testify to that from my own personal experience. But what's interesting is that, while this work demands a level of technical and clinical knowledge that goes way beyond anything we ever expected of ourselves in the past, no amount of technical expertise, whether medical or computational, is ever enough if we fail to focus on the core competency required to make this vision a reality—the skill of working with people.

The most important aspect of making our technology work better is understanding the complex matrix of views, emotions, and values people knit together into what we all collectively call the practice of medicine.

LOUIS CAPPONI, MD

Cleveland Clinic Chief Medical Information Officer

Technology-Enabled Patient and Physician Choice

As an internal medicine physician, I take care of both individual patients and patient populations, some of whom have fairly common problems, such as diabetes, hypertension, and depression, and some who have problems that aren't so common. The challenge in general medicine, unlike in a subspecialty practice where your patient mix is prescreened based on the clinician's specialty credentials, is that you never know which patient is going to present with what condition. Therefore, I need technology tools that can help me treat the broadest range of patient problems you can possibly imagine.

To do that, the EHR we're actively engaged in building will have to be able to deliver a great deal of information to clinicians and their patients in ways that make it easy for everyone to access and digest in whatever format and in whatever place they choose, whether you're connected to the Internet or not. The experience of using an EHR will need to be seamless, intuitive, and easy because, even if you don't have an Internet connection available in the moment, there will always be work that you could be doing. We'll need to access some information through the Internet, and some information will need to be contained on whatever device we prefer.

Even if the choice of device might sound insignificant compared to some of the other really big issues we are inevitably forced to confront when we think about the future of technology in healthcare, it's actually very important because people assimilate information differently, and they assimilate different kinds of information differently depending on the task and circumstance. For example, I prefer a bigger screen when I'm working with a medical chart, so I don't like looking at charts on a laptop. That's just how I work. But there are other things that I can and want to do on a smaller device, so device portability is important to me, too. It's really about making the right devices with the right interfaces available for the right purposes. When the user interface evolves to the point where the user experience is the same regardless of the platform, that's when I believe the technology will just sort of disappear into the background, which it's starting to do now, though we still have a long way to go.

When I think about the EHR we're building for the future, I see a system that will be able to store and reveal information in ways that are so digestible that it will change how we spend our time and mental energy. Unlike, say, what happens when I do a search on a standard search engine today, and I have to do that search two, three, or four times before I find what I'm looking for, which doesn't really work in the clinical environment, the promise of natural language processing that's just over the horizon will change that experience. Soon, when I do a search that's enhanced by natural language processing, my technology will answer my questions more quickly, which will allow me to spend less of my time waiting for the computer to sort through the information I need, and more of my time concentrating on the truly valuable part of a clinical encounter, which is interacting with my patient. That's what I want my technology to help me do: I want it to help me to be more present with my patients and less consumed by my computer.

At the same time that we're moving toward more real-time data processing, we also need to be thinking about the standards and workflows that will be appropriate for the kind of data access we need. I'm not just talking about published data that you can search through standard Internet sources. Clinicians absolutely *must* have access to *all* the information they need about the patient who is sitting right in front of them at this moment, regardless of where the data might have originally been captured. Today, we face a number of challenges related to how the underlying architecture and structures of our medical records might be aligned to create a national medical information exchange. We all see how many of these challenges are exacerbated by regulatory complexities that, though well intentioned, often make the documentation of care more complex than it probably needs to be. Even though we may document the care a patient receives encounter by encounter, it's the larger narrative that these encounters create that really tells the patient's story over time—it's about a lot more than just checking the right boxes.

While the discrete data/free text EHR debate is far from resolved, I would propose that simply having access to whatever electronic data is available about a patient can help me create my own a sense of that patient's narrative simply because I can see it. It's not perfect by any means, but when I can access a patient's complete record, like I did yesterday when I used the Care Everywhere[17] feature of our EHR to upload a patient's record from a facility that's 400 miles away and another facility that's 200 miles away,

LOUIS CAPPONI, MD, *continued*

which is information that previously would have taken me or my staff hours if not days to track down, if we could have found it at all, that's really powerful. Because I have access to that critical information at the touch of a button, I'm already automatically incorporating that data into my thought process, making my process all the better.

I think of that as "data orchestration," and in a business that has at its core the human relationship, I expect my technology to help me focus more of my cognitive skills on my patient. Making difficult processes simple is a big challenge. It's easy to create complexity, but it's difficult to create simplicity out of complexity. At the end of the day, that's what healthcare is really about: taking the complexity of the information and tracing it all the way down to what specific action needs to happen to help our patients get better. Our data systems need to support that activity, so they need to tax our cognitive faculties as little as possible.

Another interesting consequence of this ongoing evolution, I believe, will be the direct result of creating a technology platform that has a unified user experience across devices, for clinicians and their patients. Combined with a strong set of standards around broad data access, including how data must be formatted, recorded, and protected if it is to be included in the broader medical eco-system, I can envision a practice model that will liberate clinicians and patients from physical proximity for many of the activities related to care.

As our ability to offer patients seamless distance health and telemedicine services increases, who our patients choose for their care will become much more a function of how easy it is to access a provider virtually rather than just the proximity of a given doctor's office. Patients will also have access to very transparent information about the quality of care a given provider delivers. They'll look for providers who offer just the right level of communication and who treat them in a way that yields the best results. And they'll pick providers who make them feel comfortable about sharing the intimate secrets of their health and lives. Once they find that provider, they will be able to stay connected, even if a new job or some other event means a change in their physical circumstances.

In this model, physicians will find themselves free to practice in any way and in any location their preferences and skills support, because the content of their professional knowledge and the extent of their experience will comprise the intellectual property that makes each physician unique. Sure there will be limitations, and sure, location will matter in many situations. As our Cleveland Clinic experience demonstrates, patients will travel a long way for really important things, especially procedures. But in our envisioned future where the fundamental trust of an ongoing relationship with a physician is no longer constrained by distance, patients will get advice, tests, and even virtual exams from the provider who has the bedside manner that puts them most at ease. As patient choice increases, supported by maturing technology-enabled models of care delivery, the definition of what provider is "in network" will simply have to change.

When I think about what an EHR-enabled medical practice will look like 10 years from now, I see medicine happening much more in the home, and being highly personal. Not just personalized, but personal. Patients will have a care team that stays with them for longer periods of time, building stronger, more trusting relationships and helping to improve patient satisfaction and care outcomes. Finally, physicians or groups of physicians will have a greater ability to take their intellectual property and the way they relate to their patients and put them to use in ways that are presently constrained by geography.

As a physician, I want to work with a care team that I trust, and I want patients to experience what it's like to be part of a care team that is focused on helping them achieve their individual health and wellness goals. I want to live in a world where people aren't bankrupted by a serious health event, and where we all have access to the care we need. I'd like us all to be more productive, to live healthier, and to feel better longer. To me, the EHR and other technologies we've discussed are all about the same thing: improving the standard of our lives by improving the standard of the healthcare we receive in terms of access, cost, and the benefits we deliver across the entire population.

ROBERT WHITE, MD

Associate Chief Medical Information Officer,
Clinical Systems Office, Cleveland Clinic IT Division

Technology as Colleague and Partner

From the beginning of my career as a primary care provider, I was interested in emerging technology and how it could improve care delivery. I was always the guy who tried a technology first—what is now called an early adopter. I started doing electronic billing very early on. As the availability of technology increased and as the electronic health record became more common, it was a natural transition for me to get involved as much as I could in that way of practicing medicine.

One of the first things I recognized about the EHR was that information management was going to be the key to achieving technology's true potential. It started with things that turned out to be very hard to do, even if, at first, they sounded deceptively simple, such as placing the same kind of information in the same place every time. That's important because I believe that it's my job to create a good picture of my patient inside whatever system I'm using, not only so I can deliver the best care that I can but also so that the other providers who may be called upon to help that patient over time can do their best work, too. Knowing that I'll always find the lab results under the lab tab makes locating the information I need easier, and it does it in a way that doesn't interrupt my thought process.

I used the laboratory test result as an example because, even though I'm no expert in EHR documentation theory, it demonstrates how important it is to be fully cognizant of the relationship that clinicians have with their tools. Clinical practice is an intense experience. Even if you take all the business-related stressors out of the equation, such as not spending more time than is absolutely necessary with one particular patient while, at the same time, trying to engage in a very personal, very intimate relationship with that patient, taking care of another human being is not only a privilege, it's an enormous responsibility. It demands your attention; it demands your concentration. Physicians go to school for a long time, they work really hard, and they train and study toward that moment when the exam room door closes and they are actually practicing their art, when they're alone with their patient, focusing all of their skills on doing everything they can to help that patient overcome whatever brought him or her in. And right in the middle of that intellectual and emotional interaction—*Bam!*—we dropped in a computer. It was a gamble. That computer had to work right the first time, and every time, because the first time it didn't work right, the first time it didn't add value to the experience, it became the focus of some really intense ire. On the flip side, when it did work well, when it did add value, it became the center of an equally intense bond.

Since the late 1990s when EHRs first started appearing on the scene, and especially since about 2009 when EHR incentive payment programs and Meaningful Use regulations drove the digitization of America medicine from about a 30 percent hospital EHR adoption rate to where we are now, which is in the mid-90s, EHRs have become a lot less mysterious. Doctors are integrating the whole digital medicine concept into their thought processes, and their expectations about what the technology can do and how it can do it are increasing in sophistication at the same rate as they are integrating common "click" patterns into their muscle memory. For a lot of doctors, especially the ones who have just graduated from medical school, the way we see our clinical practice is a lot different from the view most clinicians held just a few years ago.

In 2015, at Cleveland Clinic, we exchanged nearly five million digital records, by which I mean that we used an Internet-based technology to move information either into or out of our organization as part of the coordinated care we deliver to our patients. The reason that probably sounds like a lot is because it is—and it's only going to increase over time. Driven by the digitization of healthcare, physicians are constantly resetting the bar on what we expect to be able to see about our patients and when we expect to see it.

At the same time, access to information doesn't automatically translate into understanding. As the sheer volume of the information to which a physician can connect increases, so does the clinician's need to assimilate that data into knowledge. And since there's just no way on God's green earth that, given the time I have to see a patient, I'll be able to digest all the records I could potentially access from multiple sources and multiple systems, I'm going to need some pretty impressive help.

Where do you think I'm going to look for that help?

The EHR.

The EHR of the not-so-distant future will need to bring in data from all kinds of difference source locations, and will also need to be able to help me assimilate it, understand it, and decipher it quickly. The way I see it, it won't be long until the EHR I have today will become the basic engine that will power the care I deliver. It'll do all the block-and-tackle stuff, the data capture, the routine orders, and other transactions that I need to conduct over the course of my day. On top of that, we're going to need to have a higher level of sophistication to work with information that will be coming in from other providers, from the patient, and from all the various sources connected to the Internet. It may come from population care managers, real-time journal publications, study results, or clinical trial inclusion criteria. It could be old; it could be new. But all of it, none of it, or some of it is *always* going to be important, depending on what I'm doing at that moment. That doesn't even touch the next big emerging arena of patient data, which is the genomics component, because I believe that it won't be long before genomics will be a substantial driver of what we do and don't do for our patients based on an entirely new level of understanding about their unique physiologic structures.

What I'm imagining is a kind of technology that will think with me, a kind of technology that will support my thought process and help make it—and me—more effective.

Say that I have a patient with a particular condition, what are the diagnostic tests and processes that will help me? Are there any I'm missing? Are there any I didn't necessarily think about because maybe they are only indicated in certain unusual circumstances?

I'm imagining a real-time decision-support capability that will help me make the right decision based on all the information I have at my disposal.

I'm *not* talking about taking the diagnostic decision away from the physician. Not at all. Instead, I'm imaging a scenario in which a patient tells me his or her story, I do a thorough examination, and based on what I find, I create a short diagnostic list of the conditions I think the patient might possibly have. Once I've generated that list, now I want the computer to pull everything else it can find, from every available source, to support my thinking. I want it to help me decipher it all quickly and efficiently, so that I can feel confident that I'm proceeding the right way based on facts and recorded results. Kind of like Amazon's suggestions feature that says, "Other customers who bought this also bought that." Well, all the other physicians who have collectively done this particular process a hundred million times also ordered this test. The technology would be like my "on the shoulder" consultant, available at the time I'm seeing the patient.

I think that's the direction that we need to be heading. There's just so much information out there, and finding what you need is like trying to find the proverbial needle in a haystack, while you're on the clock. If you look at the lines and lines of data that are coming into our Care Everywhere records, it's just phenomenal, and there's no way any one doctor can possibly dive into all that data and reliably find that needle.

So to me, I am going to look to my EHR to be a thinking EHR that can present information to me in a hierarchical fashion that will help me move my patients more quickly along the path to recovery. I'll also want it to help me manage not only the acute conditions I see every day, but also the common chronic conditions that affect such a large portion of the general population.

If I have a patient who is 55 years old and has a history of coronary artery disease or some other familial condition, I'll want my consulting EHR decision support tool to help me understand everything that is unique about my patient's situation and bump what I'm doing up against the best practices of my entire cohort of clinical peers. I'll want real-time risk stratification, predictive modeling that can help me educate my patients about the impact that better compliance and condition management today can have on the progression and consequences of their disease over time. And I'll want my patients to be able to use EHR-connected tools to stay connected to and to interact with the treatment plan that we devise together. That will be a really important benefit of having a thinking EHR working as part of a comprehensive preventive care strategy that can be applied to exactly the right patients at exactly the right time.

If we can build a system that's smart enough to think like a doctor and present what it knows in a way that I, as the treating physician can use, then that system is going be a game changer for everyone. If it can't, then all the additional information we can dump into the patient's record through our various exchanges is just going to be one more thing that will get in the doctor's way.

Just think about what a technology like that could do for medical research. The new knowledge it could help us discover is right there, waiting to be found, hiding in plain sight in an ocean of data that, for now, is so big that it's opaque. Ultimately, the thinking EHR could be the well-spring of our next great wave of knowledge.

To do any of those really attractive things, our thinking EHR is going to need access to a lot of important and sensitive information, information that can't be stored just any old way or accessed by just anyone. The types of information and the standards around its security and format, the interoperability of different access systems, and overall identity management—they will all be critical in establishing and maintaining the kind of trust we will all need to have in the system. Because if people don't trust the system, we simply won't use it.

I think of that place, that trusted space that will contain the collected medical knowledge of our time, as something that is very similar to the larger Internet we have today. But instead of the Wild West that is the present Internet, we're going to need a portion of the Internet to be constructed and operated in a way that will support our emerging cyber-care model. I think of it as the "Internet of Healthcare" (conceptually represented in Figure 4.2). It's something we should be thinking about very carefully now, so that we can build it right the first time, and perhaps avoid some of the delays and missteps that made the early years of the EHR go a little less smoothly than we might have liked.

FIGURE 4.2 The Next Generation of a "Thinking" EHR

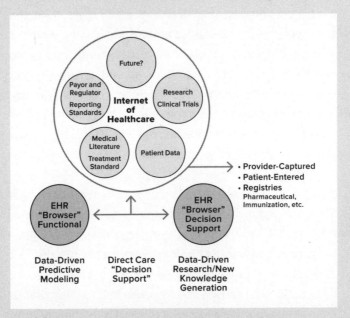

The two sides feature a basic practice engine capable of conducting daily tasks and a sophisticated, real-language-capable physician partner who will make all the information contained in the Internet of Healthcare immediately available and digestible directly at the point of care.

Beyond the Event Horizon

The details of the decisions today's health information technology professionals and their clinical partners and colleagues will be making bear precious little resemblance to the issues we overcame over a decade ago as we drew the blueprints for our integrated technology network infrastructure. Then we worried about telecom vendors and wiring diagrams on a Herculean scale. Today's architects and engineers are weighing the benefits of Wi-Fi relays and the projected market penetration and associated longevity of different smartphone platforms as the guideposts of their investment strategies. As is true with everything technology-related, the tools change quickly. So quickly, in fact, that it can occasionally feel as if some of them never really existed at all.

What is important, particularly at this moment in our history, is what Dr. Capponi called creating "simplicity out of complexity," of taking the complexity of the information and tracing it all the way down to what specific action needs to happen right now. Trying to find simplicity in a complex system is why our discussion of technology in healthcare began with the similarities between how we, as human beings, communicate with one another and organize ourselves into larger societies, and the way the Internet is organized to work. It's why it was important to note how the Internet's explosive expansion, both in terms of its sheer size and in the way people around the world use and access it, coincided with the realization that by linking what were the isolated UNIVAC-style big-brain computers that were their era's scientific marvels into connected networks that used a fairly simple set of rules to function, their power and capacity could be transformed into something that we may not, even all these years later, yet fully comprehend.

It's why I believe that technology's true value, especially in the healthcare space, can never be measured system by system, but instead must be conceptualized as being itself a system, with that system's value residing at the intersection of what existed before—how things were done, how work was accomplished, and how money was spent, and what exists after the system's switch is flipped on: how we see ourselves and our place in an organization, the details of the work we do, and the future and its potential now that so many of the basic barriers that existed between people and information are being overcome.

In many ways, healthcare is positioned, right now, precisely at the precipice of Dr. Rasmussen's event horizon.

Like the UNIVAC computer and its isolated behemoth fellows were first brought together into the first networks (CERN, ARPANET, etc.), today's healthcare and hospital systems have created their own local network structures that, though they might work well within themselves, are still predominantly insulated from one another.

As the early Internet began taking on its now-familiar shape only after the early browsers (WWW, Mosaic, Explorer, etc.) made the information it contained accessible in ways that people could understand and use, today's EHRs are beginning to take their place as the engines of clinical practice and are connecting providers and patients. Soon, they will contain all the information both providers and patients need.

The Internet only became the Internet when its various features were finally organized in a way that was both simple and flexible enough to be useful to a wide variety of people through an increasingly varied mix of devices, tasks, activities, transactions, and information that, taken together, are the fabric and form of the contemporary healthcare environment, which are beginning to exert an increasingly energetic gravitational force that is pulling the entire practice of medicine toward—what?

It is that "what" that we will explore in this book's final chapter.

SUMMARY

1. Electronic health record technology is rapidly moving beyond the limitations implicit in its name to become much more than just a record. It is being transformed by the active direction of the clinicians who use it and the efforts of IT specialists and technology vendors across the country into a dynamic connectivity tool that links clinicians to other clinicians, to their patients, and increasingly to the vast amount of patient- and practice-related data and information contained in the various systems and digital storage repository locations of which the Internet is comprised.

2. As our HIT value equation reveals, the success and tangible contributions made by a technology system must be measured not by its isolated functional capability but by the total impact the system exerts as a function of an organization's larger technical infrastructure. In this way of thinking, an EHR should not be perceived as simply a practice management system, physician order system, or documentation system. It should be understood as the single shared clinical practice space in which every provider engaged in patient care meets and works; as the repository in which all clinician orders, patient and treatment data, and a comprehensive range of practice-related information is initially captured; and as the conduit through which that information and all associated transactions will eventually flow, enabling virtually every activity, from medication prescribing to the generation of ICD-10 code-based billing statements. This more holistic view of technology components as the building blocks of an organization's cohesive functional and competitive operational infrastructure should help guide the selection of future technology systems by encouraging decision makers to respect and maintain the integrity of the total capability set they have built over time.

FIGURE 4.3 The Integrated Technology Services Value Equation (third service set)

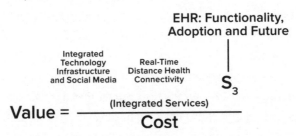

$$\text{Value} = \frac{\text{(Integrated Services)}}{\text{Cost}}$$

The third major functional category of Integrated Technology Services is an electronic health record system owned by the clinicians, administrative professionals, and patients that creates a virtual shared practice space connecting every member of a care team to the information and functional capabilities they need, whenever and wherever they are needed. It is this full set of Integrated Technology Services that taken together form the model for the emerging Internet of Healthcare that is the subject of this book's concluding chapter.

Bottom Line

The electronic health record is much more than a record. It is the dynamic, shared virtual practice space that is increasingly coming to define the contemporary healthcare marketplace in ways that are as unexpected as they are unprecedented. As today's EHRs become the common connection between clinicians, patients, healthcare provider organizations, and the larger supporting ecosystem related to medicine and medical research, the emergence of an "Internet of Healthcare" that will soon constitute a global virtual medical practice space has the potential to change how healthcare services are requested and delivered around the world. Where the Internet's strengths and weaknesses, which resulted from its very organic developmental trajectory, are often tolerated by the average user, the Healthcare Internet's success will be wholly dependent on how well the system is organized, how its information and users are kept secure, and how much its integrity can be trusted.

The Internet of Healthcare

It Only Feels Like Magic

The word *technology*, particularly in its contemporary sense, is fairly new. Generally thought to have first been used in the mid-1800s, it comes from the Greek *technologia*, which means the "systematic treatment of an art."[1] In its early English usage, it only referred to the applied arts (the process of decorating otherwise plainly rendered utilitarian objects),[2] but its definition gradually changed over time to include a growing range of ideas that all center on tools and machines. Eventually, the concept settled into what we might consider its familiar modern meaning, a "means or activity by which man seeks to change or manipulate his environment."[3] We could probably strip this definition down even further. As we use the word today, *technology* basically means a gadget; and that's the beginning of our problem because, so defined, the term loses at least half of its original sense—and the half it loses, the "systematic" part, is really important.

We all have seen it happen: a new gadget comes out, and a portion of society becomes so mesmerized by it that people are willing to stand in line for days to be among the first to possess it.[4] There is something about devices, particularly personal devices that do very specific things, that many human beings find tremendously appealing. But this is nothing new. There just seems to be something in our collective psyche that responds to the notion of designing a physical system that performs a sequential series of activities that each progressively work toward accomplishing a goal, like a machine designed to rotate a set of stones between which grain is pulverized into flour when a current of air encounters an arrangement of large, paddle-shaped blades (a windmill); or a series of carefully arranged gutters laid end-to-end over great distances, at a carefully calculated gradient, through which fresh water flows from its mountain source to a bustling city below (the aqueduct); or even a cylinder of compressed charcoal encased in a sheath of soft wood that can be filed to a point and used to scratch symbols on different surfaces to capture and record a thought (a pencil).

Then there is perhaps the greatest technology of them all: language (the actual symbols drawn by that pencil), a systematic series of specific shapes (and their associated sounds), all with agreed-upon meanings and relationships that represent both physical objects and abstract concepts, used to transfer (as accurately as the skill of the communicator will allow) the ideas that occur in one brain directly into another, not only over physical distance but across time, so that the observations, knowledge, insights, and inspirations experienced by those who live in the now can become the foundation upon which those who will follow in the future can build their world, allowing them to advance from where their progenitors left off instead of having to figure out everything afresh for themselves.

The idea is powerful: use a medium, organize a system, design a machine, create a device that does work. Build something, do something, find a pattern, analyze a relationship, learn, and pass on what you know. Can anything be more human?

The idea is so powerful that, even today, when we see a really effective piece of technology in action, it tends to feel like magic. And that was, in fact, how what we call magic may have started. Many early magicians were really creative mechanical engineers. Heron of Alexandria (c. 10–70 CE), for example, was a mathematician and inventor who created a series of water- and steam-based machines that were known as marvels in his time, including a set of temple doors that used heat and pneumatics to automatically open once a priest lit a fire on the altar. As the air inside a metal container built into the altar got hot, it expanded, forcing water from one side of a repository to another, which transferred weight to a rope that was coiled around a cylindrical lever. As the weight increased, the lever turned, causing the temple doors to open, seemingly by themselves. They remained open until the fire died down and the cooling air contracted, leaving space for the water to be siphoned back, which allowed the doors to close again, seemingly without human intervention.[5]

Or consider the "mechanical Turk," which is one of the most famous technological hoaxes in history. Created by author and inventor Wolfgang von Kempelen (1734–1804) and displayed by various owners from 1770 until it was destroyed by fire in 1854, the mechanical Turk was a life-size chess-playing clockwork doll adorned in Eastern dress that was first unveiled in the court of Austria's Empress Maria Theresa. For years the Turk toured the world, matching its mechanical wits against countless human opponents, including such notables as Napoleon Bonaparte and Benjamin Franklin. It was not until three years after the Turk was destroyed in a fire that it was finally revealed that a human chess player had been cleverly concealed inside its elaborate robotic cabinet.[6]

What is perhaps most interesting about the mechanical Turk as an example of wondrous technology is not that it actually worked, because it didn't, at least not as advertised. What is significant is how it exposed a willingness to accept the idea that a wind-up doll could actually play—and win—a game of chess against a conscious, thinking human being. Though the Turk was not a truly functioning chess-playing machine, it (he?) is credited for inspiring many inventors and thinkers over succeeding generations to try to accomplish what the robot had purportedly been able to do—a work stream that finally culminated in a project that began as a graduate dissertation at Carnegie Mellon University in 1985.

Originally called ChipTest,[7] the chess-playing machine system became a funded research initiative when graduate student Feng-hsiung Hsu and his classmate, Murray Campbell, were hired by IBM in 1989. Renamed Deep Blue, the machine was eventually matched against then world champion Garry Kasparov in 1997. Deep Blue prevailed in game six of the series, following one win by the human, one by the machine, and three games that ended in a draw.[8] Now retired, Deep Blue is one of the acknowledged inspirations of a more recent piece of technological magic: Watson, the real-language-capable query system that famously defeated two human champions on *Jeopardy!* in 2011.[9]

It is our human tendency to see technology as magical in some way that is part of its power—and its curse. When it comes to the Internet of Healthcare, the coming global medical resource that will surely emerge as its underlying infrastructure of EHRs and other integrated systems matures, we must not allow ourselves to think, even fleetingly, that the technology itself is somehow going to create its own ecosystem, unaided, unguided, and unregulated. If anything, our experience of the Internet as a whole should lead us down a different developmental pathway toward what I believe will ultimately resolve itself into a clearly delineated subportion of the broader Internet that will be controlled by a defined set of standards of acceptable behavior and data security. Yes, I said *controlled* in the same sentence that contained the word *Internet*.

While much of the Internet's success (as well as many of its resulting difficulties) can be directly attributed to the relative lack of prohibitive rules around its use and structure, I believe that the existence of a carefully created set of core rules and safeguards could, perhaps counterintuitively, free the emerging Internet of Healthcare from the constraints created by the perceived lack of security and trust that most people mention when they are asked to describe their comfort level around conducting healthcare-related activities through the World Wide Web as it exists today. For example, if you do a quick Google search for the phrase "finding credible and reliable healthcare information on the Internet," your representative results will almost invariably include cautionary phrases along the lines of the following:[10]

- Remember, anyone can publish anything they want on the Internet, whether it is true, false, or somewhere in between.

- If you come across a claim that sounds too good to be true, then it almost certainly is.

- You should always do your best to carefully analyze and research any advertising that appears on a particular website because the more you know about who and what a site will allow as an advertiser, the more you may be able to infer about the site's overall credibility.

- Always be suspicious of patient testimonials since you can never be sure that they reflect the real experiences of real people.

- Favor, when you can, well-respected, brand-name websites because, on average, they are more likely to contain the most credible information.

For the consumer, the bottom-line consensus about the reliability of most of the healthcare-related information available on many of the Internet's unregulated websites would seem to be that it is up to each of us, as individuals and potential patients, to be the final arbiters of what is true, credible, and real. It also follows that we are all pretty much on our own when it comes to making the best treatment decisions we can, based on whatever we choose to believe, however we arrive at our own personal and, most likely, less-than-strictly-scientific conclusions. In other words, buyers beware. This is not a formula for confidence.

If we return, for a moment, to the quest for simplicity outlined at the conclusion of the previous chapter, then surely there must be some better way to imagine using the amazing connectivity and communication power of the Internet to benefit those who need information and guidance as it relates to our health and well-being—which is all of us at some point in our lives.

Equally, if we begin seeing the Internet not just as an enormous, all-but-indecipherable system of uncontrollable websites but also as an existing global infrastructure for connecting to information and moving it around, for conducting transactions of various kinds—from the very basic to the dauntingly complex, and for connecting every aspect of the medical profession as it exists today in ways that will encourage and engender the creation of new structures, new organizations, and new types of medical disciplines and service providers, then we can begin to imagine a global cyber-care environment that could, one day, function like the EHR-driven shared virtual practice space Dr. Merlino described in her aspirational discussion, but on a truly impressive scale. So what should we be imagining, specifically?

We should be imagining a secure portion of the Internet that uses the web's infrastructure not only as it presently exists but as it is developing in both its speed and capacity to contain and move information, to bring patients and providers, medical practitioners and medical suppliers, medical researchers and patient advocacy groups, academics, pharmaceutical and device manufacturers, charitable outreach groups, quality-monitoring organizations, nurses, therapists, rehabilitation and assisted living facilities, hospitals, dentists, and every other direct or associated component of the contemporary medical ecosystem, including insurance providers and payors of every imaginable configuration, together into a *protected* digital practice space that is connected to thinking EHR technologies in a way that will allow us all to transcend the limitations of our current structures and discover ways of doing things that will change the way medicine is conceived and practiced in much the same way that Marconi's wireless radio transmissions changed our collective conception of distance,[11] and Einstein's ideas of relativity theory forever altered our understanding of time and space.[12]

Admittedly, that's a big statement. And who knows if any of us will actually live to see it happen?

The point is that it *can*. At least I believe it can, if we all start moving in the same direction—toward simplicity—while, at the same time, making every effort humanly possible to assiduously avoid the kind of magical thinking that might tend to encourage us to place a totally unjustified level of faith in our technology's inherent ability to design, create, or police itself.

It is, to my way of thinking, the absolute responsibility of anyone who endeavors to leverage this existing resource's largely untapped and inarguably underutilized healthcare potential to ensure that the resulting systems are engineered in an appropriate and manageable way, including the construction of built-in mechanisms that can monitor and correct automatically for any deliberate or inadvertent lapses that may impinge upon the all-important promises of security and trust that will make or break the entire domain space as a whole.

Also, we must never lose sight of the inherent need of all patients, on a human level, to connect directly with the medical professionals into whose care they place their well-being and that of those they love.

Finally, we must demand that the Internet of Healthcare, as it evolves and grows, is simple enough to be used by people with widely varying amounts of experience and sophistication, while remaining inherently flexible enough to support and encourage the kind of ongoing innovation that will lead to entirely new service categories and treatment advances about which we can only dream today, and that will only be imagined tomorrow.

So where in the world will we find a simple yet flexible model that will help us achieve these exacting goals?

Well, we've been talking about it all along, since practically the first sentences of our discussion. It's been right in front of us the entire time, so much so that it's impossible to avoid. It's the same model we've been using for decades, if not centuries. It's the doctor/patient relationship, within which there are three core concepts that comprise the cornerstones of everything the Internet of Healthcare needs to do:

1. **Trust** in a provider's commitment to patient privacy and in that provider's credentials and qualifications.

2. **Access** to the right clinician, at the right time, and to reliable information that will lead to quality decisions for both patients and providers.

3. **Value**, the kind that comes from ensuring that the monitoring, reporting, and financial structures of the practice and business of healthcare support the delivery of the highest quality care possible for every dollar invested. From building a business model that incentivizes providers to do the hard work of keeping their own practice skills up to date, their medical technology and equipment current and interoperable, and their services as affordable as possible for every patient while, at the same time, providing a compensatory level sufficient to maintain the integrity of their work and the quality of their lives.

If we all focus our attention on just these three primary attributes—trust, access, and value—I believe that a simple outline of an Internet of Healthcare that can work for everyone will begin emerging from what has, up until now, been an unintelligible jumble of undifferentiated priorities. This must be an exercise in nonmagical thinking that begins with what may at first feel like a gross oversimplification but that will (hopefully) end as a vision that is simple and flexible enough for us all to start getting our heads around.

Trust Earned, and Earned Again

Is there anything more powerful than, yet as fragile as, trust? It can take years to earn, yet in a moment, it can be lost. Without it, the simplest of relationships are doomed, yet with it, activities of almost unimaginable complexity and consequence have been contemplated and accomplished. Without it, even truth can be called suspect, and with it, even the most incredible ideas can be embraced. It can be as translucent as a veil of spiderwebs or as impenetrable as a shield of iron. Yet it is almost impossible to point to it and say, here are the

2 things, or the 5 things, or the 10 things that must always be true in order for *trust* to be shared among individuals or groups. What are those things? No one knows. We sense when they are present, and we know when they are lacking.

As it applies to the way we imagine the Internet of Healthcare, two aspects of this crucial, yet ephemeral condition we call trust will be important. The first is the trust that those functioning within the ecosystem are, in fact, who they say they are. This requirement applies to individuals, groups, patients, and providers, without exception. The second is that anyone offering information or services in a particular area of expertise is a demonstrably qualified expert in his or her chosen field.

Though I called the Internet of Healthcare a global resource, and I fully believe that it will and must be global in its ultimate scope, it will need to begin somewhere. There are perhaps as many as 1.5 billion people in the world who speak some level of English, among whom approximately 375 million are native speakers,[13] and since we are Americans participating in the American healthcare system, for us, the countries that speak English are probably a good place to start: the United States, Canada, the United Kingdom (England, Scotland, Northern Ireland, the Republic of Ireland, Wales, and the Isle of Man), Australia, New Zealand, Niger, and South Africa. English is also a primary, or at least important language in Guam, Singapore, and the Philippines, and there are many other places where English has achieved a significant level of penetration, if not societal utility.[14]

But already we begin seeing the situation. Though the language, English, may be common, the cultures, customs, currencies, and politics, even among the countries in which English is the primary linguistic infrastructure, are very different. What kind of personal identifier could possibly serve to uniquely differentiate every single individual in these varying social constructs as they access, from anywhere in the world, information and services that will be provided by individuals and organizations that will themselves reside virtually anywhere on the globe?

This brings us to an important, if somewhat nuanced, point. Though I envision the Internet of Healthcare to be an essentially "closed" environment, in that any organization or individual that is represented on real estate contained inside the confines of the domain, who uses the domain to either request or receive a service, or to conduct any type of transaction that includes personal health information or a financial transfer, will need to be authenticated, users would not need to log in to the domain for simple searches or other basic activities, such as surfing or surveying various offerings or options. A personal unique identifier for an individual would only be required to request, receive, and/or pay for a healthcare-related service, whether it is a remote second medical opinion or something that is more time-dependent, such as a real-time video consultation. Much like using Amazon's web-based retail services today, users would be free to browse all they like, but once it comes time to buy, a log-in would be required.

One exceptionally useful benefit delivered by the Internet of Healthcare, as I imagine it, would be that all the browsing a user conducts, as long as it occurs within the confines of the domain—identified by whatever dot phrase or other differentiator that successfully establishes itself as the choice of a preponderance of users—would be of trusted and trustworthy content. That would be the Internet of Healthcare's differentiating pledge. No user would ever see anything within the domain's proprietary environment that isn't authenticated. Which brings us to the authentication of healthcare information and medical service providers qualified to own and operate portions of this vision of the Internet of Healthcare.

It is extremely important to understand that I am by no means proposing, nor do I believe that it would ever really be possible, to have anyone, either as an individual or as part of some designated group, sit in judgment on the veracity or "truth" of the information providers create about subjects that fall under their professional purview, or about the efficacy of any therapeutic options providers may offer, provided that the offering does not exceed or contradict the accepted standards of their discipline. Instead, I think it will be important that among the Internet of Healthcare's founding principles is the establishment of a recognized process for verifying the authenticity of a provider's medical credentials, graduate degrees, or other licenses, and that these different qualifications are demonstrably appropriate for the work they propose to do, are recognized as sufficient by an objective governing body of expert (and most probably voluntary) representatives, are current, and are without legal or other contested infractions or encumbrances.

Just as the Internet of Healthcare will require a unique identifier that proves you are who you say you are as an individual, this secure healthcare-related Internet domain will also require that any provider of healthcare-related information and/or services must hold a recognized set of credentials that proves that they are qualified to comment on or conduct activities related to their identified area of expertise in order to qualify for authentication. How could we do something like that?

First, it will require some level of cooperation to accomplish, particularly across international borders. Though, by simply identifying the need to do it, we may actually provide an opportunity and a forum that could potentially bring groups together that have long sought similar goals but lacked a single, focused medium for their work. If we start in the United States, we have several groups that could be incredibly valuable, such as the American Medical Association, the State Medical Boards, the Federation of State Medical Boards, as well as a number of licensing and accreditation services that presently serve the needs of hospitals and other provider organizations all across the country. Also, there are many representative professional organizations, such as the American Hospital Association, the American Nursing Association, the National Community Pharmacists Association, and many others that have the kind of rich experience and deep understanding of the requirements and standards of their disciplines to contribute in a truly meaningful way to the establishment of a baseline of recognized attributes of a quality member in good standing of their respective professions.

Internationally, there are similar organizations, including the World Health Organization, the World Medical Association, and the International Federation of Pharmaceutical Manufacturers that could begin discussions around the same subjects. Across the entire European Union, questions of licensing for medical professionals crossing the borders of different member nations have been discussed for years. I am not saying that the creation of a recognized Internet of Healthcare would necessarily offer any new solutions for such longstanding legal vagaries, but perhaps the fact of the domain's existence and the potential benefits of establishing a set of rules for using it could be a catalyst to renew discussions in new and uniquely focused ways.

I recognize that this overview can start sounding utopian without some clear, real-world guardrails. But I am thinking of a domain that has a minimum number of rules for membership and use—much like the American Interstate Highway System, which was an initiative begun under the leadership of President Dwight D. Eisenhower, the former supreme commander of Allied forces in Europe during World War II, that delivered so much more than originally intended.

As supreme Allied commander, General Eisenhower had a unique perspective on logistics at a scale that was truly epic in its magnitude. Moving men and material around Europe, under combat conditions, quickly and efficiently was a defining skill for someone who would one day become responsible for coordinating the largest invasion in the history of humankind: D-day.[15] After General Eisenhower became President Eisenhower, the needs of a baby-booming generation to move around, as well as the overriding threat of the Soviet Union as a potential enemy in the increasingly tense Cold War, together made continental mobility a priority issue in the United States. Reportedly, one of General Eisenhower's most vivid memories of his time as supreme commander, after slogging his way across the cart ruts, bombed-out bridges, rubble, dust, and tangled hedgerows of Belgium, France, Italy, and the Netherlands, was of entering Germany and discovering the wonder of the Autobahn. There it was: a huge, multilane masterpiece of concrete upon which vehicles could be moved with speed and ease.

To solve America's mobility problem, particularly as it was associated with moving military assets across the country quickly, if necessary, President Eisenhower pushed for, and eventually succeeded where his predecessor, Harry Truman, had not, in moving forward with an initiative that resulted in the National Interstate Highway System,[16] which changed just about everything for America.

While the underlying incentive for connecting the country coast to coast with big, expansive ribbons of asphalt might have been ostensibly military in its vision, its result was as explosive as it was unanticipated. Along with those highways came an entire menu of new industries that all but defined American life from the late 1950s on. With highways in place, young families suddenly had places to go, which meant they needed a whole gleaming new car lot's worth of cars, campers, and vans on which they could spend the money they made following the completion of their G.I. Bill–funded educations. Once they got traveling, they needed places to stay, so the hotel industry created the now ubiquitous motor hotel, or motel.[17] Then came, for better or worse, roadside attractions, roadside advertising, and roadside places to zip in and out for some fast food—some of which was so fast, in fact, that you didn't even have to get out of your car to enjoy it. There was also overland trucking, leading to United Parcel Service (UPS), Federal Express (FedEx), and a whole industry of big rigs and bigger profits that were so big that they actually challenged the railroads for preeminence in moving freight.

The list goes on and on. The point is that by establishing a simple yet flexible common infrastructure (the Interstate Highway System's connected network of overland roads), and by creating some equally simple rules for its use (basic driving competency, including a driver's license that proved you had passed a proficiency test and were who you said you were), President Eisenhower created an engine of commerce that, almost immediately, started pumping tens of billions of dollars into the national economy and created its own subeconomy that is still driving significant value to everyone who lives in the United States, whether you drive on one of these freeways or not.

This is exactly how I envision the Internet of Healthcare's eventual impact on the business and specifics of much of medical practice. We could even stretch the analogy just a little bit further by saying that drivers (users) would never have ventured onto our new freeways, particularly into places like the great desert expanse of the country's western interior, if they didn't trust the highway map they had just bought at that last motel.

We start with trust—trust that all within the protected space of the Internet of Healthcare are who they say they are, that they know what they say they know, and that they can do what they say they can do inside a simple, flexible ecosystem that has only a few basic rules for use and enormous potential, if we understand how to *access* it.

Access, an Increase by Addition

On the Internet, access is probably most immediately associated with using a set of preauthenticated credentials to get into something—a bank account, a paid membership website, or an e-mail service. It is a twenty-first-century lock and key or, for most of us, it's a lot of locks and a big ring of invisible keys—our various passwords. That part of access is immediately and intimately tied to trust because, by its very nature, the idea of a lock implies security, protection, keeping what needs to stay in, in, and keeping what needs to stay out, out. Given that the Internet of Healthcare's ironclad commitment to trust as the foundation upon which its utility and all-important reputation will shine or collapse, the relationship between trusted identity and appropriate access when confidential information is exchanged or services rendered is the keystone that must support the weight of the entire structure.

Yet I have, to this point, consciously avoided addressing the details of what might theoretically constitute a secure user identifier that could be assigned and function across multiple sites, locations, languages, and cultures, because, quite frankly, the details just aren't really that important.

But wait, you protest. What do you mean the details aren't important? I thought you just said that the whole framework will stand or fall based on the integrity of the trusted identification system. How can the details of how you propose to accomplish that not be important? How am I supposed to trust it if I don't know what it is or how it works?

The answer lies in probability. The probability, given the realities of the modern world's hacking subculture, that any encryption algorithm we describe today, even some of those based on the mathematics of lattices, or multidimensional grids of repeating points[18] that are, depending on who you believe, either today's gold standard or a nicely complicated but already bordering-on-obsolete game of numerical cat-and-mouse, will actually be valid two months, let alone two years from now is almost precisely, and don't let anyone tell you otherwise, zippo. And even if I did have, in my possession, the Holy Grail of identity security, which would probably need to consist of a devilish combination of online password–type, user-selected letters and digits, biometrics, and some form of physical apparatus or device that could constantly be reinventing and reconfiguring itself to confound combination-generating software programs, key-morphing worm viruses, and a whole dark net's worth of other insidiously sneaky malevolents that are solely designed to get past the firewalls and other digital ramparts that are supposed to keep us safe, I certainly couldn't tell anyone about it.

No, the details aren't important, because they are absolutely going to change—regularly, and a lot. What is important is that the standards for securing a user's identity are established based on the most exacting in the industry, and that every effort is made to constantly reinforce the domain's ability to stay secure and remain as trustworthy as is humanly possible. Will encryption be 100 percent effective 100 percent of the time? Probably not. But will any breach or potential breach of a user's privacy be the result of inattention on the part of the domain's security infrastructure?

Not if the Internet of Healthcare wants to remain viable.

What is probably the more important aspect of access that should be addressed in the Internet of Healthcare's domain space actually involves data management because, though the total volume of information that will be accessible through the domain will undoubtedly be astronomical, the types of data that will need to be included are crucial as well. And while it might seem as if we are tracking back around to that big tangle of undifferentiated priorities that constitute the larger Internet, if we return to our simple patient/physician model, we will soon see that the categories of the Internet of Healthcare's data types are actually quite easy to predict.

While it may seem as if what goes on inside the exam room when you see your doctor is fairly contained, that encounter is in fact a microcosmic focal point of the entire healthcare system, in all its aspects, variations, and constructs. Your clinician is the personal product of a rigorous and exacting medical education experience, which is itself supported by a deep professional literature of peer-reviewed journals, textbooks, training systems, medical research, and other publications. He or she is fully equipped to do whatever it is that he or she was trained to do within his or her preferred practice space, from a physical examination to some minor ambulatory surgical procedures. Your clinician has a supply system supporting his or her perishable and nonperishable supply needs, access to your personal health history (electronically, we hope), nursing and other allied health support, administrative, insurance, financial, and scheduling services, and, should your situation require it, a direct line to an entire hospital-based medical care support system, including emergency medical capabilities, specialty surgeons, oncologists, hematologists, x-ray, ultrasound, and other diagnostic imaging modalities, radiation delivery devices, skilled nursing facilities, pharmaceuticals, mental health specialists, and home care services, among many others.

By using the patient/physician encounter as our model, we can quickly imagine both the kinds of information and the services that you can expect to find on the Internet of

Healthcare, and we can start outlining what kind of transactions are going to be conducted between its users and provider domain owners. While the entire ecosystem may, particularly at first, seem as if it is focusing most of its activity on helping potential patients access quality information to help guide the decisions they make about the providers who will eventually deliver whatever kind of care they need, what's important to understand is that eventually the Internet of Healthcare will become a digital mirror of the physical medical ecosystem, becoming a place in which all of the different transactions that make the businesses of healthcare run can occur. So the suppliers of medical equipment will connect to the organizations that are most likely to use their products. Pharmaceutical representatives will make e-visits to promote the strengths and differentiating aspects of their medications. And private ambulance services will coordinate their runs among the facilities they support using tracking software or real-time online logistics services offered by other Internet of Healthcare providers.

These things are obvious. What might not be so obvious will be the professional opportunities for interactions that could potentially stretch our present regulations and standards. Physician groups that provide different kinds of care that would be appropriate for a patient facing a condition with a progressive treatment schedule could theoretically decide to coalesce into a single full-service organization focused on providing that patient population total care, from diagnosis to a return home, including surgical expertise, ICU monitoring, radiation therapy, rehabilitation facilities, and even emotional recovery home care, all within the same practice. With the emerging payor preference for "bundled payment" models that provide a single reimbursement for a given condition, having control of the entire cycle of care inside a coordinated provider network or organization could be a real competitive advantage for the providers, as well as an ideal way for payors to demand and receive evidence that their money is being well spent.

What about state licensing regulations, particularly if the provider network leverages expertise located in facilities in multiple states? This is very much in line with a great deal of research that finds the best outcomes are almost invariably associated with clinicians who perform a particular activity or procedure a lot.[19] The thinking goes that the country probably doesn't need 300 complex brain tumor centers, and that, instead, we would be better served by three or four strategically located facilities that concentrate the best talent for that procedure in institutions through which a high volume of cases can be moved efficiently by clinicians who are constantly upping their game and increasing their skill.

Just in that single scenario we can see an entire laundry list of potential issues: Can state licensing requirements support distance health activities such as e-visits if patients remain in network throughout the care they receive from a national group? Will insurance providers pay for telemedicine activities as part of their standard bundled payment plans? Where would taxes be collected for services rendered by physicians who belong to groups headquartered far from the site of their current practice locations? What clinicians would be qualified to participate? Would the medical licenses or credentials granted in one state (or country) be legally recognized in another, particularly when treatment was rendered?

These are the kinds of issues that would probably be more appropriately addressed in the value portion of our Internet of Healthcare discussion, but, as is apparent, there is an interconnectivity to so many of these concepts that it is almost impossible to divide different aspects of the model into completely separate considerations. We should also think about managing all this data and all these transactions from a purely technical perspective.

Today, most hospitals and hospital systems that utilize EHR technology have their own digitally stored database of patient information. For the purposes of disaster recovery, they likely have another copy of all that data located somewhere else, just in case a catastrophe strikes their primary data center. If they offer laboratory services, they may also have two copies of all the lab-related information they generate—one in the lab and one in the EHR database—which actually means that they may have four copies of that data: one in the EHR, one in the lab, one in the EHR disaster recovery shadow database, and one in the lab's disaster recovery shadow database. If they have a picture archiving and communication system (PACS) for their radiology department, they will also have all those massive data files associated with high-resolution digital images stored in various locations.

The point is that modern medicine generates a lot of digital information—which is nothing compared to the information an even modestly functional genomics medicine department is capable of cranking out in really short order. If Twitter were architected like healthcare functions today, where every single Twitter account copied the entire portfolio of every single tweet that was ever tweeted just in case you ever want to look back and grab one, every household with a Twitter account would have a server farm in its backyard. Right now, hospitals literally copy entire databases just in case they might ever need to retrieve something from them.

If the Internet of Healthcare is going to work, it is going to need a different operating model to do so. Instead of many separate, individual databases and all the expense associated with maintaining them, not to mention the security vulnerability created by the multiple attack points multiple copies of data sets present, I imagine that we will soon see the emergence of a more service-oriented architecture through which users will call for what they need without having to store the universe of their total data sets locally. Much like a smartphone, which doesn't store or contain most of the information it delivers, when a physician or a patient wants to look up a piece of information, it will most likely be delivered through a data exchange that has a set of security and operating standards in place. This will be particularly important when patients begin utilizing our imagined medical services, traveling to get the best care within provider networks that will be required by their bundle contracts to document every single encounter, regardless of where or when it happens inside their system.

This is where cloud computing comes in. Utilizing hosted, cloud-based services through which information that adheres to agreed-upon standards of format and security can be exchanged so transparently that it becomes system agnostic can make the overall virtual practice ecosystem fundamentally interoperable and give patients complete freedom of choice and motion, as well as control over when and by whom they permit their medical information to be accessed.

How medical encounters are documented will change organically because, in this more fluid medical practice environment, documentation standards will become the common translation key that will guarantee that a medical record is comprehensible to any provider who needs to access it. Ultimately, the very pressures generated as a result of practicing medicine would become the driving catalysts for a healthcare system that will support not a preengineered experimental model but a workflow-based organization of services and activities that are directly tied to what happens inside the exam room that we used as our original model for this discussion. Which leads us to our third and final primary attribute of the Internet of Healthcare: value.

Value: What's It Worth to You?

When I related some of our experiences in rolling out an integrated EHR across the entire Cleveland Clinic enterprise in Chapter 4, I mentioned what became a very common refrain that we started hearing from many of our physician practitioners: "You know, I didn't want to make the change over to this electronic medical record system thing, but now that I'm using it, I don't know how I ever got along without it." I strongly suspect that once the Internet of Healthcare emerges into its caterpillar state, from which it will eventually be transformed into a far more impressive, colorful iteration of itself that will ultimately take wing and fly, many patients and providers will express a similar sentiment.

I started this chapter with a cautionary "magical thinking" digression for a purpose: to prevent any potential regrets. I really believe that if we don't commit ourselves to doing the Internet of Healthcare right the first time, we probably shouldn't be thinking about doing it at all.

What we can't afford to hear years from now on the other side of this transformational opportunity is, "Why didn't we do it that way in the first place?" There is so much potential value to be derived from a new, technology-enabled healthcare vision that we can't risk the disappointment and missed opportunity that would result from creating an infrastructure that no one uses.

Think about what we are really talking about.

It is said that the modern world is really tough, so tough that it can bury the aspirations of at least a portion of the population. In the old world, before instant communication over great distances and easy access to modes of transportation that moved lots of people really far really fast, the village was the center of a person's life. For centuries, people were born, grew up, married, raised their families, got old, died, and were buried—all within a radius of just a few miles. As stifling as some of us might think that sounds, it did have one distinct advantage: everyone had the chance to be the best at something, so everyone had a chance to experience the sense of self-satisfaction that comes from being recognized for doing something really, really well.

Not so long ago, to be considered a really great singer, all you needed to do was be the best singer out of the 150 or so people who lived in your village. Or you could be a really good artist, orator, organizer, or preacher because in a small town there was room for just about everybody to be good at something. Naturally, your doctor was the best—if not the *only*—doctor around.

Today, if you want to be the best singer in a particular genre, you have instant and overwhelming global competition on YouTube and the Internet and every conceivable digital streaming service you can imagine. Politicians cannot just be the best at making speeches from the back of a wagon anymore. Not only are they immediately compared to the entire recorded history of political discourse the moment they open their mouths, but portable, instant broadcast systems like Meerkat, a free, downloadable app that turns any smartphone into a live, online international news service, makes every word a politician utters in any public context instantly accessible to anybody and everybody who would like to make a comment.

While we've given up much of the comforting insularity that living within a relatively steady, moderately sized group of known individuals and their families might have offered our ancestors in years gone by, at least when it comes to the vision of an Internet of Healthcare, we are also about to give up any reason for compromise, in either the quality or personalized nature of the care we receive, because increasingly, the quality and qualities of the entire medical provider population are becoming the aggregate skill set from which we can each make our own personal healthcare choices.

If the marketplace exerts even a fraction of the distinguishing pressures around price and quality that it is purported to do, then the Internet of Healthcare has the potential of being an agent of change, indeed. Even now we are seeing fledgling retail pharmacies moving into the care delivery business, insurance companies are acquiring physician practices and establishing themselves in the access market, and hospital systems across the country are looking at one another as potential rivals, affiliates, or acquisition opportunities, depending on the mood of the marketplace that day.

For much of the foreseeable future, we will be in a transitional phase, one that promises many benefits but will also require real work. So when we think about the value we may derive from the system, we should be hanging on, as much as we can, to the "systematic" part of the original definition of the word *technology*. Each process associated with our trust and our access attributes, depending on how they are conceived and executed, will contribute significantly to the new perception of the value we experience.

As an industry and as a patient population, we must constantly be driving for a common set of trusted transactions across what will become, at first, our national, and then, ultimately, our global online healthcare environment, or there will not be a global healthcare environment at all.

One analogy is the credit card industry. Originally, credit cards were designed to work only within their own infrastructures, with the idea that if one card could gain the preferential advantage over the others, that card would crush its competition and own the entire credit card business. But the only thing that kind of hard-core competitive attitude produced was very slow growth for all the cards in the marketplace. It was not until the credit card companies agreed to a common infrastructure that they could all use to conduct their transactions that the overall value of using credit cards dramatically increased for consumers.

Suddenly, through a common infrastructure, the consumer did not have to think, "Will my card work in this store?" anymore. Instead, the number of credit cards consumers were using became dramatically unconstrained, making all credit cards more valuable and allowing the card companies to focus their services on exactly their kind of customer. Which is the good part. The not-so-good part, as we all remember, came when consumers started abusing the easy credit some card companies made available, leading to serious financial problems.

Because healthcare is based on a trusting relationship between patient and provider, we must learn from our examples so, as it relates to the Internet of Healthcare, we will never say, "Why didn't we do it that way in the first place?"

As access to care drives the need for a common infrastructure, our common infrastructure will allow us to accumulate knowledge about how we can utilize the technology to improve the ways in which care can be delivered to patients more effectively. For example, today, we have physical dialysis units both inside our hospitals and as freestanding infusion center locations. Through the Internet of Healthcare, it is not hard to imagine infusion center services diffusing all the way into the patient's home because the safest place to deliver dialysis for patients is in their home. Through the Internet of Healthcare, patients will undergo an evaluation to determine whether or not they are ready for dialysis, and if they are, it can happen locally. The decision can be made by an expert working through a central resource, with the appropriately trained visiting healthcare professional making certain that the procedure is being done correctly.

Much like our earlier eHospital example, the Internet of Healthcare has the potential to deliver similar benefits, but on a much grander scale, with reliability built directly into environment through a central knowledge base that can demand the highest level of quality control. If we consciously and systematically build a system that combines the skills of highly trained people with supporting technology-based applications, I believe we will see a change in the way care quality is measured and delivered on a global level to the point that maybe, someday, we can change "chronic disease" to "chronic wellness." We can engineer an entire care system that focuses on keeping patients healthy through coordinated virtual visits, device integration, and early detection and intervention when care is required.

It will be an incremental process, but it is already happening in some places on a broad scale, such as the Fitbit and other exercise- and wellness-oriented products, and in other places on a more focused level, such as the movement disorders home health service model Dr. Rasmussen described. Through it all, we will need to apply the scientific standards for which the healthcare industry is so rightly regarded. We need to ask hard questions about what we are doing. Can we really manage stroke at a distance? Are we really helping our Parkinson's disease patients through these technology-based services? Are we really delivering value? If so, how are we measuring it? How are we tracking it? Are we improving outcomes?

For the first time in human history, we can see a path to a real-time flow of data related to the treatment work clinicians do in a multitude of settings and locations. We can track the efficacy of a particular model or approach to care, identify false positives, calculate the frequency of interventions, and determine what we might change. What are we missing? And what are we really doing well?

If we build into the system mechanisms for constantly feeding information back into the collective accumulation of searchable, usable knowledge, making it available in an ethical way to researchers, care coordinators, quality evaluators, and the clinicians who deliver the care, what would that do to the definition of the word *value*?

As we imagine the Internet of Healthcare, that global resource that is coalescing, more or less on its own right now, but that is so powerful an idea that it is generating a kind of gravitational pull that is drawing so much of our thinking and musing in its direction, what we really should be thinking about is how we can effectively coordinate the very best of our imaginations, the very best of our private companies, and the very best of our public entities to systematically develop a secure Internet of Healthcare technology infrastructure through which we can deliver the kind of quality healthcare services that will touch and improve all of our lives.

SUMMARY

1. When imagining an Internet of Healthcare, an overall focus on three basic attributes—trust, access, and value—much like the patient/physician encounter model upon which the comprehensive vision of this potential global resource is based, can be useful in creating the lanes of work that, taken together, will ultimately make the architecture, capabilities, and utility of a secure, virtual practice space easier to understand, build, and articulate.

2. To be truly useful, an Internet of Healthcare must, first and foremost, be reliable, establishing an environment of trust that is never betrayed because, as a relationship built on the trust between a patient and a physician, any doubt in or damage done to the integrity of the experience will almost certainly translate into the entire structure's underutilization, or even its overall failure.

FIGURE 5.1 The Integrated Technology Services Value Equation Is About Patient Care

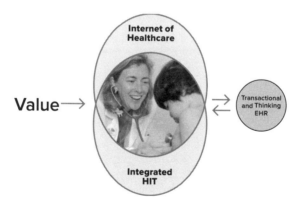

The true value of integrated health information technology systems, supported by a "thinking" EHR and coordinated to securely deliver information and services to patients and providers around the world, will be an enhanced, human connection based on trust, experience, and cooperation.

Bottom Line

The Internet of Healthcare is coming, and it is coming quickly. At present, there is little coordination of effort around the application of structure or strategy to a global virtual practice space, creating a tremendous opportunity for skilled professionals with vision, commitment, and the will to contribute in a meaningful way to the advancement of medical practice to impact the quality of the healthcare services people around the world will request and receive for many years to come.

Epilogue

Healthcare Value: The Intersection of Clinical Expertise and Advanced Technology

On Thursday, July 22, 2009, President Barack Obama arrived for a visit at Cleveland Clinic. The event was significantly different from when his predecessor, George W. Bush, visited in 2005 because President Obama did not address any large crowds while on campus. Instead, he had a brief, focused conversation with Dr. Cosgrove, then–Ohio governor Ted Strickland, and me in a small, private classroom before heading up to the Heart and Vascular Institute's fourth floor to see a demonstration of robotically assisted, minimally invasive mitral valve repair surgery. There was little fanfare associated with the presidential visit. The Secret Service did its very thorough Secret Service security sweeps, and a large tent was erected over the entrance that the president would use.

In preparation for the president's arrival, a number of Cleveland Clinic media representatives were assigned places in the national press and media access center that had been set up on the roof of the Sydell and Arnold Miller Family Pavilion, the million-plus-square-foot building that houses the Heart and Vascular Institute. The roof features a very large, glass-enclosed observation space that affords a spectacular view of downtown Cleveland. But on that morning, something kind of odd happened.

Euclid Avenue, that long stretch of road that once housed so many of America's titans of industry, runs all the way from downtown, past Cleveland Clinic to University Circle, Severance Hall (the home of the Cleveland Orchestra), the Cleveland Museum of Art, Case Western Reserve University, University Hospital, the Cleveland Museum of Natural History, and on into Euclid, Ohio, an inner-ring suburb of Cleveland that shares the grand old avenue's name. Given its length and prominent placement as Cleveland's main east-west artery, Euclid Avenue is normally quite busy, regardless of the time of day. But today, it was empty. Not a car was visible in either direction as far as the eye could see.

Then, way off in the distance, first one, and then two, and then a whole line of tiny black spots materialized, crawling in a long, slow line past the Terminal Tower east, approaching Cleveland Clinic's old white hospital. It was a motorcade, a rolling phalanx of shiny black SUVs, probably a dozen in all, one after the other, with the lead and last blinking alternating flashes of red and blue from within their large front grilles. As they approached, three black military-style helicopters swept in from three different directions, aligning themselves in a perfect, rotating circle above the narrow length of green space in front of the J building where the president would soon disembark.

Another unusual feature of the president's visit was, for us, perhaps even more memorable than the visit itself. It happened the day before the president arrived. In the days leading up to the visit, no matter who asked, the White House had refused to say why the president had decided to visit Cleveland Clinic. He was actually scheduled to give a healthcare policy–related speech at a local east side high school later in the day, so stopping in to see us was obviously not the point of the trip. But still, when asked about the reason for visiting Cleveland Clinic, the White House press people stubbornly remained silent. And everyone knows how much the media loves silence.

The White House's silence stoked public speculation regarding the "real" reason the president had decided to put Cleveland Clinic on his itinerary for the day. Remember, Cleveland Clinic is an internationally recognized leader in all things heart care, a reputation our clinicians have earned and kept for decades. Our cardiothoracic surgeons, cardiologists, cardiology researchers, and cardiovascular thought leaders are influential members of the medical community, and our present Cardiovascular Medicine department chair, Steven Nissen, MD, just two years before, in 2007, had been recognized among *Time* magazine's "100 Most Influential People," along with former U.S. Vice President Al Gore, Queen Elizabeth, and director Martin Scorsese.[1] 2007 was also the year that a Heart and Vascular Institute team led by Tomislav Mihaljevic, MD, announced that it had successfully used a "beating heart" transplant device that was able to keep a donor heart warm and beating during transport, an innovation that promised to shorten transplant wait times and broaden the geographic availability of donor hearts.[2] Dignitaries, politicians, Hollywood stars, and even members of the Saudi royal family had famously made Cleveland Clinic their provider of choice for heart care for years.

So if you were going to speculate about the reason a sitting U.S. president might want to pay a visit to Cleveland Clinic, what would be the first thing that would pop into your head?

Interestingly, that's not what happened. Instead, a prominent local newspaper, admitting that the White House was declining to state what the president was interested in talking about at Cleveland Clinic, decided to guess. And they guessed that what the president wanted to talk about was not heart care. It was technology.

In the four years since President Bush's visit, the work we had been doing at Cleveland Clinic around health information technology, electronic health records, and everything else associated with the digitization of our medical practice had gone from a subject so obscure that we had been asked to think of explaining it to a population who had never so much as thought about such things before to, at least in this circumstance, our organization's front-of-mind distinguishing differentiator in a news reporter's front-page speculations.

We thought that was kind of a big deal because it indicated to us that technology in healthcare had become a priority topic. The public was beginning to recognize its importance. Policy makers were focusing in on how to encourage its use. And clinicians were getting personally and deeply involved in making sure it worked right for what they needed it to do.

We did in fact talk about our HIT capabilities with President Obama, and the mitral valve surgery repair demonstration he watched was conducted using a robot.

In the years since that visit, the work has progressed. Technology has gotten better. And the vision of a technology-enabled medical practice model that so powerfully motivated our work when we first started years ago was no longer confined to those of us "in the business." It's about time. In other industries, such as banking or retail, the Internet seemed to just rush in and wipe all the pieces off the board, starting an entirely new game before anyone knew what was happening. But healthcare is an inherently conservative activity, as it should be, because there really is no such thing as a noninvasive medical encounter. Even having your doctor tell you to take an aspirin is, in reality, the considered recommendation of a trained healthcare professional that you introduce a measured quantity of a specific chemical directly into your body. So in a business in which the consequences of your actions are manifested in the physical body of another human being, you'd better be conservative. You'd better be sure that the things you are saying and doing are right, proper, and proven. So, sure, clinicians are sometimes a little slow to adopt new things just for the sake of adopting them.

But as our discussion has demonstrated, in just a few short years, we have, as an organization, a profession, and a country, gone from simply plugging in a computer and seeing how it might work in a doctor's office to imagining an entire global Internet of Healthcare infrastructure that is not, repeat, *not* a dream. It's going to happen. And it's going to happen soon. So we all need to pay attention and stay focused on ensuring that our progress is thoughtful, systematic, and positive. Which brings us to one final point.

At the start of Chapter 5, we saw how, in 1997, Deep Blue, the chess-playing machine developed at IBM, defeated world champion Garry Kasparov. When the machine beat the human at what many maintain is the quintessential human game of skill, logic, strategy, planning, cunning, and foresight, there were many who lamented the toppling of mankind from the pinnacle of the evolutionary heap. There were even those who insisted that we were seeing our first glimpse of the life form that would one day supplant us as the dominant sentient consciousness on the planet. There have long been science fiction stories that predict the eventual rise of computers as humankind's most dangerous competition, with artificial intelligence assuming the role of our Promethean fire that, once created, inevitably consumes its maker. There are nightmarish but, at least up until that moment, fictitious books, movies, and prognostications from thinkers great and greater stretching back for generations. But never before had there been an actual, discernible, provable event toward which anyone could point and say, "There! There is the seed of our extinction. There, in that darkness, is hidden our dire future!"

Until that day in 1997 when a piece of software bested the chess master and defeated our human champion, categorically, undeniably, and publicly, through cold, analytical, data-driven, calculation-based logic.

Or not.

Recently, during an interview with statistician and writer Nate Silver, one of Deep Blue's original designers, Murray Campbell, revealed that the reason Deep Blue beat Garry Kasparov was probably because of a bug in the software. As the story goes, during the course of the game, Deep Blue made a move that just did not make a lot of sense. Suspecting that the machine had formulated some deep and subtle strategy that he was unable to comprehend or adequately visualize, Kasparov's subsequent decisions lost some of their sharpness, and the game simply slipped from his grasp. But the move that was interpreted at the time by some of the world's most experienced chess masters as sophisticated on so refined a level as to be suspicious to the point that some called foul, claiming that there just had to be, much like the Mechanical Turk centuries before, a secret human hand at work was, according to Murray Campbell, a guess.

That's right. Apparently, the way Deep Blue's software was written was that if, after a certain number of calculations, no clearly preferred move was identified, which was what must have happened in this case, the system was designed to simply select a move at random.[3] So that oh-so-sophisticated, devastatingly strategic move that is credited by some as the lethal stroke that beat Garry Kasparov was, in fact, a guess.

It was a simple human work-around, written directly into the rules that comprised the mind in the machine that beat the human being, and not some omniscient, unfathomable mathematical consciousness communing with the irrepressible clockwork soul of Newton's eternal universe.

The machine couldn't make up its mind, so it took a chance.

There is, in that revelation, a kind of beauty. Technology is not magic, and it is not separate from its creator. Technology is an extension of people, and one way that people extend and express themselves is through the technology they make. If, as many artists insist, part of the creator's soul is woven into his or her work, animating it with whatever energy possessed the creator in that moment of inspiration, then health information technology should have, somewhere in its architecture, a measure of the compassion and concern for the well-being of others that drove the computational artisans who brought it into being.

Technology will never be perfect because the people who make it will never be perfect. But if we are unwavering in our commitment to ease the suffering of others and to make their lives more comfortable, their fears less frequent, and their futures, in some measure, more securely their own; if we can express, through the things we do and the responsibilities we satisfy, our passion for making every tool we have and every tool we imagine work for the good of us all, then health information technology professionals, medical professionals, and everyone engaged in this work should proudly see—like the amazing ability to make a guess that its programmers wrote into Deep Blue's operational code—a little bit of ourselves in the machines we make and the machines we use to take care of one another.

Notes

Introduction

1. G. W. Bush: "Remarks to the American Association of Community Colleges Convention in Minneapolis, Minnesota," April 26, 2004. Online by Gerhard Peters and John T. Woolley, The American Presidency Project. http://www.presidency.ucsb.edu/ws/?pid=72610.
2. The Yale Center for Dyslexia and Creativity, Delos "Toby" Cosgrove, MD, biography, 2015, Yale School of Medicine, 333 Cedar Street New Haven, CT, 06510.
3. D. Cosgrove, LinkedIn, https://www.linkedin.com/pub/toby-cosgrove/58/941/760.
4. The White House Archives, http://georgewbush-whitehouse.archives.gov/news/releases/2005/01/20050127-2.html.
5. J. Cummings, "The Benefits of Electronic Medical Records Sound Good, but Privacy Could Become a Difficult Issue: As Most People Know Nothing About EMRs, Public Opinion Will Be Strongly Influenced by Reports—Whether Good or Bad—in the Media," Harris Interactive, February 8, 2007.
6. K. Fonkych and R. Taylor, *The State and Pattern of Health Information Technology Adoption* (Santa Monica, CA: RAND, 2005).
7. R. Hillestad, J. Bigelow, A. Bower, F. Girosi, R. Meili, R. Scoville, and R. Taylor, "Can Electronic Medical Record Systems Transform Health Care? Potential Health Benefits, Savings, and Costs." *Health Affairs* 24, no. 5 (September 2005): 1103–1117.
8. J. H. Bigelow et al., *Analysis of Healthcare Interventions That Change Patient Trajectories* (Santa Monica, Calif.: RAND, 2005).
9. "Germ Theory," Encyclopædia Britannica, http://www.britannica.com/topic/germ-theory. Accessed August 24, 2015.
10. S. O. Zandieh, K. Yoon-Flannery, G. J. Kuperman, D. J. Langsam, D. Hyman, and R. Kaushal, "Challenges to EHR

Implementation in Electronic-Versus Paper-Based Office Practices," *Journal of General Internal Medicine* 23, no. 6 (June 2008): 755–761. (Published online March 28, 2008, doi: 10.1007 /s11606-008-0573-5. PMCID: PMC2517887.)

11. I. Rutkow, *Seeking the Cure: A History of Medicine in America* (New York: Scribner, 2010), 169.
12. In 1892, Dr. Crile performed what was perhaps the first total laryngectomy in the United States; in 1913 he was a cofounder of the American College of Surgeons; and in his lifetime he wrote more than 20 medical books.
13. J. A. Balgrosky, *Essentials of Health Information Systems and Technology* (Burlington, MA: Jones & Bartlett Learning, 2015), 86–87.
14. Health Information Management Systems Society (HIMSS) Board of Directors, "What Is Interoperability?" April 5, 2013, http://www.himss.org/library/interoperability-standards/what -is-interoperability.
15. Health Evolution Partners, Inc., Team, www.healthevolution partners.com.
16. U.S. Department of Health & Human Services, HITECH Act Enforcement Interim Final Rule, http://www.hhs.gov/hipaa/for -professionals/special-topics/HITECH-act-enforcement-interim -final-rule/index.html.

Chapter 1

1. http://my.clevelandclinic.org/services/heart/disorders/aortic -aneurysm/hic_Abdominal_Aortic_Aneurysm.
2. http://www.webmd.com/heart/picture-of-the-aorta.
3. A. Maton, J. Hopkins, C.W. McLaughlin, S. Johnson, M. Quon Warner, D. LaHart, and J. D. Wright, *Human Biology and Health* (Englewood Cliffs, NJ: Prentice Hall, 1995).
4. http://www.ncbi.nlm.nih.gov/pubmedhealth/PMHT0023062/.
5. http://my.clevelandclinic.org/services/heart/disorders/aortic -aneurysm/hic_Abdominal_Aortic_Aneurysm.
6. Medtronic Patient Information Booklet, *Endovascular Stent Grafts: A Treatment for Abdominal Aortic Aneurysms* (Santa Rosa, CA: Medtronic, 2013), 2.
7. http://my.clevelandclinic.org/services/heart/disorders/aortic -aneurysm/hic_Abdominal_Aortic_Aneurysm.
8. Levester Kirksey, MD, Staff, Department of Vascular Surgery, Cleveland Clinic Heart and Vascular Institute.

9. Pew Research Center, "Internet User Demographics: As of January 2014, 87% of American Adults Use the Internet," http://www.pewinternet.org/data-trend/internet-use/latest-stats/.
10. E. Dougherty, "What are Thoughts Made Of? They're Really Just Electro-chemical Reactions—but the Number and Complexity of These Reactions Make Them Hard to Fully Understand." The MIT School of Engineering, April, 2011, http://engineering.mit.edu/ask/what-are-thoughts-made.
11. Stanford University, "Bits and Bytes," CS101, Introduction to Computing Principles, https://web.stanford.edu/class/cs101/bits-bytes.html.
12. P. Miller, "How Much Is 1GB, and What Does It Mean?" Karma Mobility Inc., https://blog.yourkarma.com/how-much-is-1GB.
13. Cisco Systems, "The Zettabyte Era: Trends and Analysis," White Paper, May 2015, http://www.cisco.com/c/en/us/solutions/collateral/service-provider/visual-networking-index-vni/VNI_Hyperconnectivity_WP.pdf.
14. The Endowment for Human Development, "Grasping Large Numbers," http://www.ehd.org/science_technology_largenumbers.php.
15. J. Brownlee, "Google Books Calculates the Total Number of Books Ever Written at Almost 130 million," Geek, August 6, 2010, http://www.geek.com/news/google-books-calculates-the-total-number-of-books-ever-written-at-almost-130-million-1275493/.
16. http://percentcalculator.com/?gclid=CKOitKKYkMoCFQoKaQodaKkMBg.
17. L. St. Amour, "The Internet: An Unprecedented and Unparalleled Platform for Innovation and Change," The Global Innovation Index, 2012, World Intellectual Property Organization (WIPO), http://www.wipo.int/edocs/pubdocs/en/wipo_pub_gii_2012-chapter10.pdf.
18. F. F. Marvasti and R. S. Stafford, "From Sick Care to Health Care—Reengineering Prevention into the U.S. System," New England Journal of Medicine 367 (September 6, 2012):889–891, doi:10.1056/NEJMp1206230.
19. M. Smith, "Breaking The Enigma Code Was the Easiest Part of the Nazi Puzzle: The Brilliant Minds at Bletchley Park Cracked an Even Greater Set of Secrets, the Lorenz SZ40 Code." The Telegraph, November 15, 2014, http://www.telegraph.co.uk/history/world-war-two/11231608/Breaking-the-Enigma-code-was-the-easiest-part-of-the-Nazi-puzzle.html.

20. C. Saran, "Apollo 11: The Computers That Put Man on the Moon," ComputerWeekly.com, http://www.computerweekly.com/feature/Apollo-11-The-computers-that-put-man-on-the-moon.
21. G. Gensosko, *When Technocultures Collide: Innovation from Below and the Struggle for Autonomy* (Waterloo, ON, Canada, Wilfrid Laurier University Press, 2013), 51.
22. Oxford English Dictionary, "fractal," Oxford University Press.
23. Dictionary.com, http://dictionary.reference.com/browse/fibonacci+sequence.
24. M. Bourne, "Golden Spiral," SquareCircleZ, the IntMath Blog, September 4, 2011, http://www.intmath.com/blog/mathematics/golden-spiral-6512.
25. P. Mohanty, R. C. Malik, and E. Kasi, *Ethnographic Discourse of the Other: Conceptual and Methodological Issues* (Newcastle, UK: Cambridge Scholars Publishing, 2008), 22–23.
26. L. Barrett and P. Henzi, "The Social Nature of Primate Cognition," *Proceedings of the Royal Society* 272, no. 1575 (September 2005).
27. M. Konnikova, "The Limits of Friendship," *New Yorker*, October 7, 2014.
28. Q. D. Atkinson, "Phonemic Diversity Supports a Serial Founder Effect Model of Language Expansion from Africa," *Science* 332, no. 6927 (April 15, 2011): 346–349.
29. W. J. Bernstein, *Masters of the Word* (New York: Grove Press, 2013), 17.
30. Effective Language Learning, "Language Difficulty Ranking," http://www.effectivelanguagelearning.com/language-guide/language-difficulty.
31. Ibid.
32. N. Jerry, *Chinese* (Cambridge: Cambridge University Press, 1988).
33. Nations Online, "Most Spoken Languages in the World," http://www.nationsonline.org/oneworld/most_spoken_languages.htm.
34. S. Barnes, "Second Languages Spoken by Countries Around the World," My Modern Met, November 6, 2014, http://www.mymodernmet.com/profiles/blogs/second-languages-of-the-world-infographic.
35. E. D. Reilly and W. L. Langer, *Concise Encyclopedia of Computer Science* (New York: John Wiley and Sons, 2004), 825.
36. J. Koplin, "An Illustrated History of Computers," The Oxford Math Center, Oxford College of Emory University, Oxford,

Georgia, 2002, http://www.oxfordmathcenter.com/drupal7
/node/11.

37. Atomic Heritage Foundation, "Computing and the Manhattan
Project," http://www.atomicheritage.org/history/computing
-and-manhattan-project.

38. M. Bellis, "The History of the UNIVAC Computer: John
Mauchly and John Presper Eckert," About.com, http://
inventors.about.com/od/uvstartinventions/a/UNIVAC.htm.

39. T. Jones, "Dewey Defeats Truman," *Chicago Tribune*, July
13, 2008.

40. L. R. Johnson. Coming to Grips with Univac, Annals of the
History of Computing," *IEEE* 28, no. 2 (April–June 2006): 32,
42, doi:10.1109/MAHC.2006.27.

41. R. Alfred, "Nov. 4, 1952: UNIVAC Gets Election Right, but CBS
Balks," Wired.com, http://www.wired.com/2010/11/1104cbs-tv
-univac-election/.

42. Ibid.

43. D. Hernandez, "Killer Bits: This Real-Life Supercomputer
Inspired HAL 9000, the Evil AI from '2001: A Space Odyssey,'"
Fusion, April 25, 2015, http://fusion.net/story/125819/this-real
-life-supercomputer-inspired-hal-9000-the-evil-ai-from-2001-a
-space-odyssey/.

44. Dictionary.reference.com.

45. Ibid.

46. As a side note, there is an interesting urban legend that
maintains that the name "HAL" was actually a one-letter
-ahead cipher for IBM, a claim that Arthur C. Clarke, author of
the book series Space Odyssey, from which the movie took its
inspiration, denied.

47. University System of Georgia, "A Brief History of the Internet:
Sharing Resources," http://www.usg.edu/galileo/skills/unit07
/internet07_02.phtml.

48. W. Mulzer, "The Making of the World Wide Web," Freie
Universitat, Berlin, http://www.inf.fu-berlin.de/lehre/SS01/hc
/www/www2.html.

49. Ibid.

50. The Linux Information Project, "GUI Definition," October
2004, http://www.linfo.org/gui.html.

51. P. Kaushik, "Radar Displays," *International Journal of
Innovative Research in Technology* (IJIRT), Volume 1, Issue 7,
2014, http://www.ijirt.org/vol1/paperpublished/IJIRT101324_
PAPER.pdf.

52. Doug Engelbart Institute, "Living History, the Engelbart Archive," http://www.dougengelbart.org/.

53. World Heritage Encyclopedia, "History of the Graphical User Interface: 2.3 Apple Lisa and Macintosh (and later, the Apple IIgs)," World Heritage Encyclopedia, Article ID WHEBN0000013914, World Public Library, 2016, http://central.gutenberg.org/articles/history_of_the_graphical_user_interface#Apple_Lisa_and_Macintosh_.28and_later.2C_the_Apple_IIgs.29.

54. S. Gibbs, "From Windows 1 to Windows 10: 29 years of Windows Evolution," *The Guardian*, October 2, 2014, http://www.theguardian.com/technology/2014/oct/02/from-windows-1-to-windows-10-29-years-of-windows-evolution.

55. C. Anderson, "The Man Who Makes the Future: Wired Icon Marc Andreessen," *Wired* magazine, April 2012, http://www.wired.com/2012/04/ff_andreessen/.

56. S. Thill, "March 17, 1948: William Gibson, Father of Cyberspace," *Wired* magazine, March 2009, http://archive.wired.com/science/discoveries/news/2009/03/dayintech_0317.

57. L. H. Newman, "Netscape Navigator, Everyone's First Browser, Turns 20 Today," *Slate*, October 2014, http://www.slate.com/blogs/future_tense/2014/10/13/netscape_navigator_browser_created_by_mosaic_communications_corporation.html.

58. J. Daly and C. Winkler, "A Visual History of Internet Explorer," *StateTech* magazine, August 2013, http://www.statetechmagazine.com/article/2013/08/visual-history-internet-explorer.

59. K. Dunn, "The First Great Internet Browser War, Internet Browser Review, "September 2015, http://internet-browser-review.toptenreviews.com/the-first-great-internet-browser-war.html.

60. B. Widder, "Battle of the Best Browser: Edge vs. Chrome vs. Firefox vs. Safari vs. Opera vs. IE," *Digital Trends*, September 2015, http://www.digitaltrends.com/computing/best-browser-internet-explorer-vs-chrome-vs-firefox-vs-safari-vs-edge/.

61. C. Bailey, "Chances Are You Spend Way Too Much Time Staring at Screens Every Day," A Life of Productivity, July 10, 2014, http://alifeofproductivity.com/chances-spend-way-much-time-staring-screens-every-day/.

62. A. Grush, "New Study Claims Smartphone Addiction Is Similar to Drug Addiction," Android Authority, September 16, 2015, http://www.androidauthority.com/smartphone-addiction-drug-642320/.

63. D. Pierce, "We're on the Brink of a Revolution in Crazy-Smart Digital Assistants," *Wired*, September 16, 2015, http://www .wired.com/2015/09/voice-interface-ios/.

64. A. Russo, "Internet2: It's better, it's faster. You can't use it," *Slate*, June 7, 2005, http://www.slate.com/articles/technology/ webhead/2005/06/internet2.html.

65. M. E. Porter and E. O. Teisberg, *Redefining Health Care: Creating Value-Based Competition on Results* (Boston: Harvard Business School Press, 2006).

66. F. R. Cockerill, "Cleveland Clinic Healthcare Quality Innovation Summit," Group 6B, Laboratory Medicine and Pathology Service, Mayo Clinic, May 5, 2011.

67. K. Crow, "Value Analysis and Functional Analysis System Technique," Product Development Management Association and the Engineering Management Society, DRM Associates, 2613 Via Olivera, Palos Verdes, CA 90274, 2002.

Chapter 2

1. Internet Society, "Internet Society Global Internet Report, 2015: Mobile Evolution and Development of the Internet," 9.

2. Ibid.

3. E. Marcotte, "Responsive Web Design," A List Apart, May 25, 2010, http://alistapart.com/article/responsive-web-design.

4. A. Zimmerman Jones, "Observer Effect," About Education, About.com, http://physics.about.com/od/physicsmtop/g /ObserverEffect.htm.

5. B. D'Espagnat, P. Eberhard, W. Schommers, and F. Selleri, *Quantum Theory and Pictures of Reality* (Berlin, Germany: Springer-Verlag Berlin and Heidelbert Gmb H& Co. KG, 1989).

6. "Gap Analysis," BusinessDictionary.com, http://www.business dictionary.com/definition/gap-analysis.html.

7. All logo issues were resolved in 2005 with the adoption of Cleveland Clinic's current logo and branding system, which is applied with uniform rigor across all Cleveland Clinic facilities, signage, vehicles, wearables, websites, and identification around the world.

8. The Cleveland Historical Team, "Millionaire's Row," Cleveland Historical, a project by Center for Public History and the Digital Humanities, http://clevelandhistorical.org/items /show/10.

9. Massachusetts Court System, "The Red Scare of 1919–1920: Causes of the Red Scare," http://www.mass.gov/courts/court-info/sjc/edu-res-center/saco-vanz/the-red-scare-of-1919-1920-4-gen.html.
10. BBC History, "Nicholas II (1868–1918)," 2015, BBC.com, http://www.bbc.co.uk/history/historic_figures/nicholas_ii.shtml.
11. J. Marion, "Best of Breed or Single Vendor—Which Is Right for Healthcare Imaging? Which Environment Can Best Meet Clinician Needs and Still Achieve Meaningful Use Compliance?" *Healthcare Informatics* (*HI*), August 23, 2013, http://www.healthcare-informatics.com/blogs/joe-marion/best-breed-or-single-vendor-which-right-healthcare-imaging.
12. Cleveland Clinic Information Technology Division, Clinical Systems.
13. Cleveland Clinic Information Technology Division, Clinical Systems Office.
14. Cleveland Clinic Information Technology Division, Technology Services
15. Psychology Dictionary, "What Is Self-Image?," http://psychologydictionary.org/self-image/.
16. J. P. Hewitt, *Oxford Handbook of Positive Psychology* (Oxford: Oxford University Press, 2009), 217–224.
17. A. N. Katz, "Self-Reference in the Encoding of Creative-Relevant Traits," *Journal of Personality* 55, no. 1 (1987): 97–120, doi:10.1111/j.1467-6494.
18. S. C. Holub, A. M. Haney, and H. Roelse, "Deconstructing the Concept of the Healthy Eater Self-Schematic: Relations to Dietary Intake, Weight and Eating Cognitions," *Eating Behaviors* 13, no. 2 (April 2012): 106-111.
19. Franklin D. Roosevelt, Inaugural Address, March 4, 1933, as published in Samuel Rosenman, ed., *The Public Papers of Franklin D. Roosevelt, Volume Two: The Year of Crisis, 1933* (New York: Random House, 1938), 11–16. (This phrase was part of a speech written, as were many of FDR's speeches, by Raymond Moley.)
20. K. Vallotton, *How Heaven Invades Earth: Transform the World Around You* (Ada, MI: Baker Books, 2013); quotation of P. K. Bernard.
21. K. Casey, *Change Your Mind and Your Life Will Follow: 12 Simple Principles* (Newburyport, MA: Conari Press, 2008).
22. Team members include Cora Liderbach, Tyler Maddox, Nicole McClain, Stephanie Petrucci, Kaye Spector, and Michelle Wallace.

Chapter 3

1. AHA/ASA Guidelines, "Guidelines for Prevention of Stroke in Patients with Ischemic Stroke or Transient Ischemic Attack: A Statement for Healthcare Professionals from the American Heart Association/American Stroke Association Council on Stroke," *Stroke* 37 (2006): 577–617.

2. D. Brady, "Mobile Stroke Units Shaving Crucial Minutes off Response Times in Texas, Ohio," *Washington Post*, To Your Health, February 11, 2015, https://www.washingtonpost.com /news/to-your-health/wp/2015/02/11/mobile-stroke-units -shaving-crucial-minutes-off-response-times-in-texas-ohio/.

3. American Heart Association, American Stroke Association, "Ischemic Strokes (Clots)," August 7, 2015, http://www.stroke association.org/STROKEORG/AboutStroke/TypesofStroke /IschemicClots/Ischemic-Strokes-Clots_UCM_310939_Article .jsp#.Vo_72U-FOig.

4. American Heart Association, American Stroke Association, "Stroke Treatments," May 23, 2013, http://www.stroke association.org/STROKEORG/AboutStroke/Treatment/Stroke -Treatments_UCM_310892_Article.jsp#.Vo_4Zk-FOig.

5. W. Barlow and D. Powell, "A Dedicated Medical Student: Solomon Mordecai, 1819–1822," *Journal of the Early Republic* 7.4 (1987): 377–397.

6. L. F. Wolper, *Physician Practice Management: Essential Operational and Financial Knowledge*, 2nd ed. (Burlington, MA: Jones & Bartlett Learning, 2013), 11.

7. I. Dixon, "Civil War Medicine: Modern Medicine's Civil War Legacy," Civil War Trust, October 29, 2013, http://www .civilwar.org/education/history/civil-war-medicine/civil-war -medicine.html.

8. W. Hering, "A Year of the X Rays," *Popular Science Monthly* 50 (March 1897): 654; published online August 23, 2015, https:// en.wikisource.org/wiki/Popular_Science_Monthly/Volume_50/ March_1897/The_Year_of_the_X_Rays.

9. W. Welch, "The Hospital in Relation to Medical Science," *Journal of the American Medical Association* 59 (1912): 1668.

10. I. Rutkow, "Seeking the Cure: A History of Medicine in America" (New York: Scribner, 2010) 108–111.

11. C. Baldwin, "Chronology: Key Dates for Texas Businessman Ross Perot," Reuters, September 21, 2009, http://www.reuters .com/article/dell-perot-systems-idUSN2128118420090921.

12. Ibid.

13. J. Stern, "Dell Buys Ross Perot's IT Service Company for $3.9 Billion," Sept. 21, 2009, *Gizmodo*, http://gizmodo.com/5364178/ dell-buys-ross-perots-it-service-company-for-39-billion

14. S. Hansell and A. Vance, "Dell to Spend $3.9 Billion to Acquire Perot Systems," *New York Times*, September 22, 2009.

15. HIMSS, "About HIMSS: Frequently Asked Questions About HIMSS and Its Members," http://www.himss.org/himss-faqs.

16. PewResearch Center, "Home Internet Access, Percent of American Adults Who Access the Internet via Dial-up and Broadband," PewResearch, http://www.pewresearch.org/data -trend/media-and-technology/internet-penetration/.

17. The National Telecommunications and Information Administration, "A Nation Online: How Americans Are Expanding Their Use of the Internet," 2002, https://www.ntia .doc.gov/legacy/ntiahome/dn/html/Chapter3.htm.

18. A slightly renamed Epic product.

19. Also an Epic product.

20. An Epic product as well.

21. Cleveland Clinic Heart and Vascular Institute, "Diseases and Conditions, What Is Pectus Excavatum?," http://my.cleveland clinic.org/services/heart/disorders/hic_pectus_excavatum.

22. L. Kalanithi, W. Tai, J. Conley, T. Platchek, D. Zulman, and A. Milstein, "Better Health, Less Spending: Delivery Innovation for Ischemic Cerebrovascular Disease, Comments and Opinions," *Stroke* 45 (2014): 3105–3111.

23. "Event Horizon: Black Hole," *Encyclopaedia Britannica*, School and Library Subscribers, 2016, http://www.britannica.com /topic/event-horizon-black-hole.

Chapter 4

1. The Famous People Society for Recognition of Famous People, "Famous People: Scientists, William Osler Biography," http:// www.thefamouspeople.com/profiles/william-osler-127.php.

2. "The William Osler Papers, 'Father of Modern Medicine': The Johns Hopkins School of Medicine, 1889–1095," U.S. National Library of Medicine, National Institutes of Health, https:// profiles.nlm.nih.gov/ps/retrieve/Narrative/GF/p-nid/363.

3. "History of The Johns Hopkins Hospital, Johns Hopkins: The University's Founder," The Johns Hopkins University, The Johns Hopkins Hospital, and Johns Hopkins Health System, http://www.hopkinsmedicine.org/Medicine/hstrainingprogram /overview/hx_jhh.html.

4. Agency for Healthcare Research and Quality, "Observing Patient Care Rounds: CUSP Toolkit, Communication Among Disciplines Can Be Improved If Viewed Through the Eyes of an Objective Observer," U.S. Department of Health and Human Services, http://www.ahrq.gov/professionals/education /curriculum-tools/cusptoolkit/toolkit/obsrounds.html.
5. "What Does SpO2 Mean? What Is a Normal SpO2?," Withings, Inspire Health, October 29, 2015, https://withings.zendesk.com /hc/en-us/articles/201494667-What-does-SpO2-mean-What-is-a -normal-SpO2-level-.
6. J. Leggett, "History of Mobile Phones," uSwitch Mobiles, November 3, 2015, http://www.uswitch.com/mobiles/guides /history-of-mobile-phones/.
7. "The History of Cell Phones," Tech-FAQ, Independent Media, 2016, http://www.tech-faq.com/history-of-cell-phones.html.
8. Ibid.
9. R. Ritchie, "History of iPhone: Apple Reinvents the Phone," August 31, 2015, iMore, Mobile Nations, http://www.imore .com/history-iphone-original.
10. Mojave Media Group, edited by L. Richter, "A Brief History of the Blackberry," Bright Hub, October 14, 2009, http://www .brighthub.com/office/collaboration/articles/8041.aspx.
11. P. Savage, "Designing a GUI for Business Telephone Users," *Interactions* 2, no. 1 (January 1995): 32–41, DOI=http:dx.doi .org/10.1145/208143.208157.
12. Ibid.
13. L. Jacobs, "Interview with Lawrence Weed, M.D.—The Father of the Problem-Oriented Medical Record Looks Ahead," *The Permanente Journal* 13, no. 3 (Summer 2009): 84–89.
14. K. Pinkerton, "History of Electronic Medical Records," Ezine Articles, July 2006, http://ezinearticles.com/?History-Of -Electronic-Medical-Records&id=254240.
15. Adele Goldberg, ed., *A History of Personal Workstations*, (Reading, MA: Addison-Wesley, 1988).
16. N. Farber, "The Law of Attraction Revisited: It's the Principle of the Thing," *Psychology Today*, January 5, 2014, https://www .psychologytoday.com/blog/the-blame-game/201401/the-law -attraction-revisited.
17. Epic Systems Health Information Exchange platform technology.

Chapter 5

1. Dictionary.com, "technology," in Online Etymology Dictionary. Source location: Douglas Harper, Historian. http://www.dictionary.com/browse/technology. Available: http://www.dictionary.com/. Accessed: June 09, 2016.
2. "Applied Art: Definition and Meaning," Encyclopedia of Art Education, http://www.visual-arts-cork.com/definitions/applied-art.htm.
3. Ibid.
4. L. Petrecca and E. Weise, "Buyers Swarm Apple Stores for iPhone 5," *USA Today*, September 23, 2012.
5. M. Shuttleworth, "Heron's Inventions," Explorable.com, https://explorable.com/heron-inventions.
6. L. Davis, History's Greatest Robot Hoaxes, http://io9.com/5053731/historys-greatest-robot-hoaxes, iO9.com.
7. IBM, "The Making of Deep Blue," https://www.research.ibm.com/deepblue/meet/html/d.3.1.html.
8. IBM, "Deep Blue: Transforming the World," IBM100, http://www-03.ibm.com/ibm/history/ibm100/us/en/icons/deepblue.
9. J. Markoff, "Computer Wins on 'Jeopardy!': Trivial, It's Not," *New York Times*, February 16, 2011, http://www.nytimes.com/2011/02/17/science/17jeopardy-watson.html.
10. Trisha Torrey, "Finding Credible, Reliable Objective Health Information on the Internet," Verywell, updated June 16, 2014, https://www.verywell.com/finding-credible-health-information-online-2615425.
11. "Guglielmo Marconi: Physicist, Inventor, Entrepreneur (1874–1937)," Biography.com, http://www.biography.com/people/guglielmo-marconi-9398611.
12. Max Planck Institute for Gravitational Physics, "Elementary Einstein," Einstein Online, 2016, http://www.einstein-online.info/elementary.
13. "The Most Spoken Languages Worldwide (Speakers and Native Speakers in Millions)," Statista: The Statistics Portal, 2016, http://www.statista.com/statistics/266808/the-most-spoken-languages-worldwide/.
14. "English Around the World," 5 Minute English, 2013, http://www.5minuteenglish.com/english-around-world.htm.
15. J. A. Warren, "D-Day Was the Largest and One of the Bloodiest Invasions in History," *The Daily Beast*, June 6, 2014, http://www.thedailybeast.com/articles/2014/06/06/d-day-was-the-largest-and-one-of-the-bloodiest-invasions-in-history.html.

16. "Why President Dwight D. Eisenhower Understood We Needed the Interstate System," U.S. Department of Transportation, Federal Highway Administration, https://www.fhwa.dot.gov /interstate/brainiacs/eisenhowerinterstate.cfm.

17. "Motor hotel," The Free Dictionary by Farlex, http://www.the freedictionary.com/motor+hotel.

18. N. Wolchover, "The Tricky Encryption That Could Stump Quantum Computers," *Wired*, September 19, 2015, http:// www.wired.com/2015/09/tricky-encryption-stump-quantum -computers/.

19. M. E. Porter and T. H. Lee, "The Strategy That Will Fix Health Care," *Harvard Business Review*, October 2013, https://hbr .org/2013/10/the-strategy-that-will-fix-health-care.

Epilogue

1. M. O'Riordan, "Dr. Steve Nissen named to *Time* magazine's '100 Most Influential People,'" May 3, 2007, Medscape, News & Perspective, http://www.medscape.com/viewarticle/789270.

2. "2007 Year in Review, Clinical Achievements, Seeing Things Differently," Cleveland Clinic 2007 Annual Report, https:// my.clevelandclinic.org/ccf/media/Files/About/CC_Annual_ Report_2007.pdf?la=en.

3. K. Finley, "Did a Computer Bug Help Deep Blue Beat Kasparov?" *Wired*, September 28, 2012, http://www.wired .com/2012/09/deep-blue-computer-bug/.

Index

Abdominal aortic aneurysm ("triple A"), 16–21
Access, Internet of Healthcare, 172, 180–186
Addiction, smartphone, 35
Advanced Research Projects Agency Network (ARPANET), 32
Alberts, Jay, 109
Andreesen, Marc, 34, 35
Apple, 34, 124
ARPANET (Advanced Research Projects Agency Network), 32
Artificial intelligence, 199–200
AT&T, 123
Augmentation Research Center, 34
Authentication, 175–180

Babylonia, ancient, 30
Base stations, 123
Bedside manner, 151
Berners-Lee, Tim, 32–33
Best-in-breed, 57–58, 61
Bit, 22
Blackberry, 124
Brailer, David, 11–12
Brand/branding, 72
Browsers, 33–37
Bundled payment model, 183–184, 186
Bunts, Frank Emory, 5
Bush, George W., v, ix, 1, 11–12, 195
Byte, 22

Campbell, Murray, 168, 200
Capponi, Louis, 147–152, 161
Care Everywhere, 149–150
Carnegie Mellon University, 168
CBS (Columbia Broadcasting System), 31–32

CERN (Conseil Européen pour la Recherche Nucléaire), 33
Champion, physician, 130–131
Charts, paper (see Paper medical records)
Chess, 167–168, 199–200
ChipTest, 168
Civil War, 85
Cleveland Clinic:
  main campus, 51–52
  national branches, 52
  origins of, 4–6, 51
Cleveland Clinic Global Patient Services, 92
Cleveland Clinic Heart and Vascular Institute, 15–16, 195
Cleveland Clinic Telestroke Network, 79, 101–103
Clinical space, 110–112 (See also Shared practice space)
Clinical Systems Office, 138, 146
Cloud computing, 186
Cognitive therapy, 64–65
Columbia Broadcasting System (CBS), 31–32
Computers:
  human development parallels, 27
  and Internet, 26–27
  origins and early evolution, 30–31
  pre-Internet history, 26
Congestive obstructive pulmonary disease (COPD), 119–120
Conseil Européen pour la Recherche Nucléaire (CERN), 33
Content marketing, 70
Cosgrove, Delos "Toby," 2, 54, 61, 195
Credentials, Internet of Healthcare and, 176
Credit cards, 92, 189–190

Crile, George W., 4–7
Cyberspace, 34

Data, narrative vs., 128
Data exchange, 186
Data orchestration, 150
Deep Blue (computer), 168, 199–200
Department of Defense, U.S., 32
Device, choice of, 147–148
Dewey, Thomas E., 31
Digital data, current shortcomings
    of, ix
Digital ecosystem, 45, 49, 68–69
Disaster recovery, 185
Distance Health, 100–101, 108
Documentation, 142–143, 149
"Doorbell," 119
DrConnect, 96, 134
Dunbar, Robin, 28–29

E-Cleveland Clinic, 86–97
eCleveland Clinic, 96–97
eCleveland Clinic DrConnect, 96
eCleveland Clinic MyChart (see
    MyChart)
eCleveland Clinic MyPractice (see
    MyPractice EHR)
eHospital:
    ICU Monitoring Center, 117–119
    MyPractice EHR, 122–123
    nurses' attitudes towards, 120–121
EHR (see Electronic health record)
Eisenhower, Dwight D., 31, 177–179
Electronic health record (EHR):
    Cleveland Clinic's rollout of,
        129–139
    EMR vs., 37
    evolution of, 125–127
    as healthcare's primary enabling
        function, 37
    as shared practice space, 140–141
    Lawrence Weed's contributions to,
        127–128
    (See also Electronic medical record
        [EMR])
Electronic medical record (EMR):
    as common "browser" of medical
        practice, 37
    EHR vs., 37
    Epic®, 60, 80

hypothetical use case, 8–11
and information flow, 7–8
inpatient vs. outpatient orientation
    of, 56, 60
introduction of plan at Cleveland
    Clinic, 2–3
meaningful use, 12
One Cleveland Clinic initiative,
    55–56
patients as most important
    beneficiary of, 7
potential benefits, 2–3
(See also Electronic health record
    [EHR])
Employees, One Cleveland Clinic
    mission and, 65
EMR (see Electronic medical
    record)
English language, 174–175
Enterprise identity, 61–62
Epic® (electronic medical record),
    60, 80
Epic rollout project, 131
Etiquette, physician, 141
Event horizon, 110, 111

FaceTime, 20
Family Health Centers, 58
Fibonacci sequence, 28
Fogelman, Adam, 60
Foreign languages, 30
4G wireless, 124
Fractals, 27–28
Franklin, Benjamin, 167
Free text (medical record content),
    128, 149
Functional value (healthcare value
    equation element), 39

Gap analysis, 49
Gibson, William, 34
Gigabyte, 22
Golden spiral, 28, 29
Graphical user interfaces (GUIs),
    33–35
Guzman, Jorge, 116–122

HAL 9000, 32
Handheld devices, 35
Harris, C. Martin, 60, 91

Health Essentials and Social Media team, 69
Health Essentials blog, 70
Health Information Management Systems Society (HIMSS), 90–91
Health information technology (HIT):
  need for clear definition, 38
  value equation for, 24, 38–39
  value of system as functional whole, 40
Health Information Technology for Economic and Clinical Health (HITECH) Act, 11–12
Healthcare Internet technology (HIT), 37
Heart and Vascular Institute (Cleveland Clinic), 15–16, 195
Heart murmurs, 98–100
Heron of Alexandria, 167
HIT (*see* Health information technology)
HITECH (Health Information Technology for Economic and Clinical Health) Act, 11–12
Home, as location for health care, 152
House calls, 85
Hsu, Feng-hsuing, 168

ICU (intensive care unit), 116–122
Identifier/ID number (*see* Personal identifier)
"In network," 151
Industrialization, 85
Information, understanding vs., 129
Information management, 153
Infrastructure, Internet of Healthcare, 190
Inpatient care, EMRs and, 56, 60
Integrated EHR, 39–40
Integrated Technology Services Value Equation, 75, 114, 164, 193
Intensive care unit (ICU), 116–122
Interfaces, 33–35, 57, 148
Internal expert resource, 145
Internal medicine, 147
Internet:
  current use for health information searches, 21

expansion of traffic volume since 1992, 23
GUIs and, 33–35
origins of, 32–33
reasons for power of, 24
as starting place for health information, 22
and travel, 36–37
vetting of healthcare information on, 169–170
volume of digital data on, 22–23
Internet browsers, 33–37
Internet Explorer, 35
Internet of Healthcare, 159–160, 165–194
  access, 172, 180–186
  authentication of information, 175–180
  browser, 111–112
  core concepts, 172–173
  HIT and, 24
  licensing, 184
  personal identifiers, 174–175
  rules/safeguards, 169–170
  trust and, 172–180
  value, 173, 187–192
Internet Protocol (IP), 32
Internet2, 36
Interstate Highway System, 177–179
Intravenous tissue plasminogen activator (tPA), 82–83
Intubation, 121–122
IP (Internet Protocol), 32
iPhone, 20, 124
IT professionals:
  integration with other healthcare stakeholders, 24
  introduction of technology by, 141–142
  and needs of clinical colleagues, 59

Jensen, Karen, 97–98, 100
Jobs, Steve, 124
Johns Hopkins Hospital (Baltimore, Maryland), 115

Kasparov, Garry, 168, 199, 200
Katzan, Irene, 77–83

Kempelen, Wolfgang von, 167
Kirksey, Levester, 20
Kubrick, Stanley, 32

Laboratory tests (see Test results)
Language:
  origins of, 29–30
  as technology, 166
Leonardo da Vinci, 30
Licensing:
  and Internet of Healthcare, 177,
    184
  and remote second opinion
    process, 89
"Live chat," 15–16, 21
Livengood, Bridget, 71
Logging, 135
Logging in (Internet of Healthcare),
  175
Loop, Floyd, 55–56
Lower, William Edgar, 5–7
"Lunch and learns," 131

Macintosh computer, 34
Magic, technology and, 167, 168
Making rounds, 115–116
Maria Theresa, Empress of Austria,
  167
Marketing:
  E-Cleveland Clinic, 92–95
  healthcare vs. traditional, 67
  One Cleveland Clinic, 65–73
Marketing and Integrated Web
  Services team, 66–67
Martin, Bill and Bonnie, 15–21
Matsen, Paul, 65–68, 72
Meaningful Use, 12, 129, 154
"Mechanical Turk," 167–168
Medical Center Hospital of
  Vermont, 128
Medical records, paper (see Paper
  medical records)
Medical research, 158–159
Merlino, Amy, 140–146
Mick, Stephanie, 99, 100
Microsoft, 34, 35
Mihaljevic, Tomislav, 197
Mobile devices:
  history of, 123–124
  MyChart and, 136

as website design driver, 46–47
  (See also Smartphones)
Mobile Stroke Treatment Unit,
  78–81, 83, 103–107
Morris, William, 126–127
Mosaic browser, 34
Motorola DynaTAC 800X, 123
MyChart, 96, 132, 134–137
MyChart eNewsletter, 135
MyConsult, 86, 96, 99
MyPractice EHR, 78–80, 83, 96, 97,
  118, 122–123, 134–135

Napoleon Bonaparte, 167
Narrative, data vs., 128
National Institutes of Health Stroke
  Scale (NIHSS), 81–82
Natural language processing, 148
Netscape Navigator, 35
Networking:
  Cleveland Clinic framework and,
    60–61
  power of, 30–33
911 calls, 105
Nissen, Steven, 197
Numbers, language and, 30
Nutrition consultations, 95

Obama, Barack:
  2009 visit to Cleveland Clinic,
    195–198
  on Cleveland Clinic's health IT
    system, v
  and HITECH Act, 12
Observer effect, 48–49, 55
Omori, Sue, 88
"One Cleveland Clinic" initiative,
  49–63
  background, 49–54
  enterprise identity, 62–63
  Family Health Centers, 58
  IT infrastructure issues, 57–62
  origins of, 49–50
  patient care as core of, 56–57
  patient identifier system, 55–56, 60
  perception-oriented tasks for,
    64–65
  self-examination of organization,
    55
  standardization, 54

Online marketing, 65–73
Online portal, 96
oNLine System, 34
Organizational psychotherapy, 48
Osler, Sir William, 115
Outpatient care, EMRs and, 56,
   60

PACS (picture archiving and
   communication system), 185
PAG (Physician Advisory Group),
   131, 138
Pancreatitis, 135–137
Paper medical records, 3, 52–54
Parkinson's disease, 109
Partin, Mary, 59–60
Patient identifier (see Personal
   identifier)
"Patients First" promise, 67
Perot, Ross, 90, 91
Perot Systems, 90
Personal identifier:
   inpatient vs. outpatient
      orientation, 60
   and Internet of Healthcare,
      174–175, 180
   and One Cleveland Clinic
      initiative, 55–56
Phillips, John, 7
Physician Advisory Group (PAG),
   131, 138
Physician champions, 130–133
Piar, Pam, 58–59
Picture archiving and
   communication system (PACS),
   185
POMR (problem-oriented medical
   record), 128
Porter, Michael, 39
Posk, Lori, 137
Practice space (see Shared practice
   space)
Preadoptive consultations, 95–96
Pregnancies, high-risk, 140
Presidential elections, 31–32
Primary care, 153
Probability, Internet security and,
   181
Problem-oriented medical record
   (POMR), 128

PROMIS (Problem-Oriented
   Medical Information System),
   128

Quality (healthcare value equation
   factor), 39
Quality control, 191
Quantitative Health Sciences, 119

Railway Medicine, 85
Rasmussen, Peter, 101–104, 108–110,
   124
Raymond, Daniel, 100
Real-time data processing, 149
"Red box," 118, 121
Red Scare (1919–1920), 51
Regional hospitals, 120–121
Remington Rand, 31
Research, medical, 158–159
Research in Motion (RIM), 124
Responsive design, 47
Return on investment (ROI), 40
Riley, Monte and Sandy, 98–100
RIM (Research in Motion), 124
ROI (return on investment), 40
Rounding (making rounds), 115–116

Safety, standardization and, 54
Schaffer, Jonathan, 87
Search engines, 21, 148
Second opinions, 19, 88–92, 102–103
Security:
   Internet of Healthcare, 180–182
   MyPractice EHR, 135
Self-esteem, 63–64
Self-image, 63
Self-schemas, 64–65
Shared practice space:
   EHR as, 140–141, 143, 145–146,
      164
   Internet of Healthcare as, 159,
      170–172
Shreen, Deb, 135–137
Silver, Nate, 200
Simplicity:
   complexity and, 150, 161
   and Internet of Healthcare,
      171–172
Smartphones:
   addiction to, 35

evolution of, 124–125
and Telestroke, 102, 120
tremor app, 109
Social brain hypothesis, 28
Social groups, size of, 29
Social media, 69–72
State licensing requirements, 184
Stevenson, Adlai, 31
Strickland, Ted, 195
Stroke, 77–83, 101–104
Sydell and Arnold Miller Family
    Pavilion, 195
Systems, technology and, 165–167

TCP (Transfer Control Protocol), 32
Technology:
    as colleague/partner, 153–160
    history of, 165–168
    language as, 166
    origin of term, 165
    true value of, 139, 161–162
Teisberg, Elizabeth, 39
Telemedicine kiosks, 120
Telestroke, 79, 101–103
Test results, 135–137, 153–154
Thinking EHR, 157–160, 171, 193
Third-party vendor, internal expert
    resource vs., 145
3G wireless, 124
TIA (transient ischemic attack), 77
Todorovich, Amanda, 69–71
Touch screens, 46
Transfer Control Protocol (TCP), 32
Transformation, EHR and, 138–139
Transient ischemic attack (TIA), 77
Translator concept, 142, 144–145
Travel, Internet's effect on, 36–37
Truman, Harry S., 31, 178
Trust:
    in current healthcare information
        on Internet, 169–170

EHRs and, 159
Internet of Healthcare and,
    172–180
"Trusted source" information, 68
Turk, Joe, 91
Twitter, 71
2001: A Space Odyssey (film), 32

Understanding, information vs.,
    129
Unique/user identifier (see Personal
    identifier)
UNIVAC (Universal Automatic
    Computer), 31–32
University of Vermont, 128
USA Today, 93–94

Value:
    eHospital program and, 120–121
    Internet of Healthcare and, 173,
        187–192
    marketing, 67
    of technology, 139, 161–162
Value equation:
    for HIT, 24, 38–40
    Integrated Technology Services,
        75, 114, 164, 193
Virtual shared practice space (see
    Shared practice space)
Voice interfaces (VIs), 35

Watson (computer), 168
Web browsers, 33–37
Website design, 45–48, 95–96
Weed, Lawrence L., 127–128
White, Robert, 153–160
Windows operating system, 34
Winners, Stacey, 104–107
Wireless phones, 123
World Wide Web (WWW), 26–27,
    33 (See also Internet)

About the Authors

C. Martin Harris, MD, is the chief information officer and chairman of the Information Technology Division of Cleveland Clinic, where he is also a staff member in the Department of General Internal Medicine. Dr. Harris is the executive director of eCleveland Clinic, a series of secure, online technology-enabled clinical programs and services.

In his role as chief information officer, Dr. Harris is responsible for implementing information technology strategies that support the clinical and business objectives of Cleveland Clinic. He is a member of the eHealth Initiative Leadership Council, where he works to eliminate hurdles to the development of the ehealth marketplace. He was a member of the Association of American Medical Colleges Better Health 2010 Advisory Board and an advisor to the National Committee for Quality Assurance on the confidentiality of patient information.

He serves on the President's Commission on Interoperability, the Certification Commission for Healthcare Information Technology, and the National Institutes of Health Advisory Committee to the Director; he also served on the Health Information Technology (HIT) Standards Committee of the Department of Health and Human Services, and was a presidential appointee on the President's Commission on Care for America's Returning Wounded Warriors.

Dr. Harris received his undergraduate and medical degrees from the University of Pennsylvania. His residency training in general internal medicine was completed at the

Hospital of the University of Pennsylvania. He also completed a Robert Wood Johnson Clinical Scholar fellowship in general internal medicine at the University of Pennsylvania School of Medicine and holds a master's degree in business administration in healthcare management from the Wharton School of the University of Pennsylvania.

Gene Lazuta is the senior director of strategic communication at the Division of Information Technology at Cleveland Clinic and its Secure Online Services program. He has worked at Cleveland Clinic in various capacities since 1995. He has written numerous research and white papers, magazine and online articles, and book chapters. A graduate of Baldwin-Wallace University, he is the author of 10 novels.

Put the Cleveland Clinic Way to Work for You